The Forming Process

By: David Edmondson

*Founder and CEO of Covenant Connections Church
International and DE Ministries.
Senior Pastor of Covenant Connections Church, Flowery
Branch, Ga.*

Published by

CHRISTIAN DAY
Publishing Co. ™

The Forming Process
Copyright © 2012 by David Edmondson

Cover design by Jerry Leaphart
Author photo on cover by Christian Randall

Unless otherwise noted, scripture quotations are from the King James Version of the Bible.

Published by Christian Day Publishing Company
P. O. Box 1836, Flowery Branch, GA 30542

ISBN 978-0-9827486-1-9

Printed in the United States of America
2012 – First Edition

CONTENTS

Acknowledgements

My wife Stephanie: Thanks for sticking by me through it all. You are my helpmate and my love.

David Edmondson

Dedication

I would like to dedicate this book to my Dad, John David Edmondson Sr., who passed away in 1998 of cancer. Even though he had his struggles, addictions and faults, he was my Daddy and for that I love him. It is because of who my Dad was, as well as who he wasn't, that I can know my Heavenly Father the way I do today. I have learned that all the times Daddy wasn't there for me, Father was. I love you, Daddy.

Editor's Note

This book has been edited in a light fashion to preserve the unique voice of the author. Colloquialisms and unusual grammatical structures are integral to the character and personality of the author's ministry of teaching and preaching, and therefore have been retained. It is our sincere hope the result will communicate a realistic impression of the passion and down-to-earth tone that is part and parcel of the author himself.

Foreword

Do you know how God really created you?

Do you know God had a destiny for you before He created you?

Do you know you were equipped by God to fulfill your destiny before you ever entered this world?

If you do, this book may not be for you.

On the other hand, if you cannot answer yes to each of these questions, and you are willing to take a few minutes to learn, the truths in this book will mold and shape you, and enable you to see yourself as God sees you!

Come, and together we will take a journey into the creative mind of God – not just relative to the creation of the man, Adam, but the creative process of God's design for you, specifically.

* * *

It is very important for us to understand the process whereby we were created. Knowing and understanding the creative structure by which God creates us will bring security, wisdom, faith, and an assurance that God has a plan and purpose for you in particular.

I believe that the most traveled road of the enemy is the way of making you lose, forget or never understand your God-created purpose in life. Think for just a moment about all the times in your life you have felt alone, frustrated, unworthy, lost, undone, no good or even worthless. Where do those feelings come from? We know by reading the Word of God, the Bible, that these feelings do not come from God.

In Jeremiah 29:11 the Lord says:

"For I know the thoughts that I think toward you, saith the LORD, thoughts of peace, and not of evil, to give you an expected end."

Here, God is telling you that when He thinks of you His thoughts are always good and peaceful. The Psalmist said His thoughts of us are precious and innumerable (Psalms 139:9, Psalms 40:5). God's thoughts are also to instill in you His purpose for your life. "...to give you an expected end." The Hebrew word from which "expected" is translated also means "the thing that is longed for."

I am sure that we can face and overcome any obstacle in this world if we have the answer to this question. *Why am I here at this time, created in this way, and for what purpose?*

The devil will create havoc in your life and make you think the destruction he inflicts is God's will. Or the devil will wrap your lack of purpose in superficial coverings such as, "you're not smart enough;" "God hates you," or "your grandparents and parents were poor, sick and worthless, so you are destined to live and die the same as those before you."

All these lies are overshadowing the root problem, and that is that you don't know or understand the way God thinks of you, according to your created purpose or destiny.

We are created to solve problems. In Genesis 1:27-28, the Bible says God created man in His image and gave him the Earth, to subdue it and have dominion over everything on it. That means God instilled in mankind the abilities to solve any problem and handle any situation on this Earth through His Spirit that is in us.

We are problem solvers. That is in the creative makeup of mankind. So when troubles arise in our lives, this creative part of us immediately begins to try and solve the problem.

Yet, we often fail to live up to our destiny because we tend to deal with the "fruit" of our problem and not the "root" of our problem.

This is so important; I need to say it once more: **people often fail to live up to their destinies because they tend to deal with the "fruit" of their problems instead of the "root" of their problems**.

Have you ever read the account in the Bible where Jesus cursed a poor little fig tree? (Mark 11) There is an underlying truth in this account that I would like to share with you, so let's look at it for a moment.

Jesus and His disciples were walking down the road and Jesus saw a fig tree that had leaves on it, but it was not producing figs. Then, we read that, "It was not time for figs yet."

Well, I asked the Lord one day, why, in all of His wisdom and understanding of the times and seasons, did Jesus go to get figs off of a fig tree that had no figs? Why also did Jesus curse this poor tree that had produced no figs when it wasn't even its season to produce figs? So I read up on the cycle and make-up of fig trees and learned, to my surprise, an incredible revelation of God's character when dealing with out-of-control problems. See, the interesting thing about the productive cycle of fig trees is that during their season to produce, they put forth figs first, and then leaves. So what caught Jesus' eye was that this fig tree was out of sync with its purpose or creative cycle. If it had leaves, it should have had figs. There was a problem.

Now the way we would solve this problem is by pruning the surface abnormality – just whack off what we can see is wrong, guessing that the problem is in the makeup of the leaves and branches. But Jesus knew that what He saw on the surface was not the problem, but the real problem was in the roots of the tree. So Jesus cursed the fig tree "from the root up." (verse 20)

I said all of that to say this. A lot of times we kill ourselves pruning the dead fruit in our lives when in reality the only true way to solve a problem is to deal with the root. I believe that the root of most of our problems is the loss of our God-created purpose!

So now you see the reason for this book. My desire is for you to read this book, study the references in the Bible, and allow yourself to see and love yourself the way God sees and loves you. It all begins in the beginning!

Let's get started!

Making History,
Pastor David Edmondson

PART ONE

The Reason for Mankind
[The Truth of Our Creation]

A Gift of God's Image:

"Then God said, 'Let us make man in our image, in our likeness, and let them rule over the fish of the sea and the birds of the air, over the livestock, over all the earth, and over all the creatures that move along the ground.'"
Genesis 1:26

———

Some of the proudest moments in my life are those times when I am with my son or daughter and someone remarks how they look like me. I love to hear how much my children look like me because, after all, I have the prettiest and most handsome children in the world. Pride swells within my heart to think that my wife and I had a small part in creating two incredible children.

Though my son is only ten at this time and my daughter is seven, I look into their eyes and fall in love with them every day. As I watch them, see their mannerisms and hear their phrases, I can't help but see myself in them.

There is no greater creative joy than seeing your image in your children. This is the platform from which God desired to create mankind: so he could look upon His creation (Earth) and upon His image (Mankind). The proudest moments in the infinite life of God are when He looks down on His creation (Earth), even as it has been destroyed by sin and rebellion, and He gazes upon His creation (Man), even through all the sin, death, and hurt, and still see Himself in us. One thing that blows my mind is the fact that God looks past everything that I do that reflects the opposite of Himself, and, through His love for me, chooses to search for His image in me. This process is called "grace," the same grace He extends to us through His Son Jesus Christ.

This world we live in operates on image. How others see you is how they will treat you. Knowing this, we fall into a deadly cycle of performing to please. See, if we let it, our human flesh will set aside who we are, our morals and what we believe just to portray an image pleasing to those around us.

The fact of the matter is, we all live in the same fallen world and we all get caught up in the same image-chasing dead-end road.

Let me go ahead and let you in on something.

All those people you are living to impress with a fake, polished image – they are going to drop you like a bad habit when you fail to perform! If you have lived in this world for more than a few years, you have probably experienced what I am talking about. Working to please and failing anyway is a vicious cycle. Experiencing and seeing the doomed-to-failure nature of that cycle can drive you to close off those around you and even the true image inside you. It can cause you to stop trying to succeed. "Taking a chance" toward achieving your dreams will become just a phrase crushed under the weight of hurt, rejection and the past. Soon, you will stop seeing yourself as the image of God and you'll begin to mistake yourself for who you think you ought to be.

"Why can't I have a good relationship with God?" This is the question you'll ask yourself while blaming God for not creating you like someone you think has it all together.

How can you have a relationship with someone you blame for your lack of "perfection"? How would you feel if your child came up to you and said, "Dad and Mom, I don't like looking like you"?

I know that, for me, it would be very devastating. I would be crushed to know my image was rejecting me because the world said he or she should look different.

Before you go any further, you must understand that God can and does look through all of your shortcomings and imperfections and says, "That's my boy (or girl)!"

The question is, can you do that? Can you look through those shortcomings and imperfections and see the image of God in yourself? You have His word that it is there.

If you read the Foreword of this book, you saw that in Jeremiah 29:11 the Lord says:

> *"For I know the thoughts that I think toward you, saith the LORD, thoughts of peace, and not of evil, to give you an expected end."*

What we must recognize as we begin this journey is the fact that, for all practical purposes, you cannot change how God sees or thinks of you, for He sees the real, inner you that He created in His image. His thoughts toward you are peace – which, in the meaning of the Hebrew word used there for peace, means "health, prosperity, rest and safety" among other related good and desirable situations.

. What you can change, though, is how you see yourself. You can begin to see yourself the way God sees you and, thereby, see more clearly the wonderful "expected end" He wants for you.

God knows who I really am and He knows nothing can destroy or change His image in me! The fact of the matter is, if my children were to be adopted, change their hair color, or even move to another land and culture, they would still have my image. They would just be called by a different name, live in a different land, and have roots that need to be colored every month. But wherever they may go and whatever physical change they may try to make, my image will always be there and undergird them.

Thank God that when I mess up, act a fool, or maybe even turn my back on God, He never forgets my true image! No matter what comes my way, nothing can change whose image I am created in.

If the truth were known, God's love allows Him to be attracted to His image in me, even when His image is camouflaged by my misfortunes and mistakes.

Isn't God wonderful?

You cannot achieve God's love by work. He doesn't want you to perform to be accepted by Him. The decision has already been made. His image has already been given. The only factor left to be decided is whether you are going to accept the facts He sees.

I know what you are thinking: this is too good to be true! God loves me for who I am?

Yes, He does! God loved you enough to create you to resemble Him. Why else would He send His only begotten Son to save you, except through His great love for you? Every day as you walk this Earth, God is in heaven saying, "Angels, Cherubim, come quick! Those are my children! Aren't they awesome?"

Remember Romans 8:38 & 39 say, *"For I am persuaded, that neither death, nor life, nor angels, nor principalities, nor powers, nor things present, nor things to come, nor height, nor depth, nor any other creature, shall be able to separate us from the love of God, which is in Christ Jesus our Lord."*

"Performing is portraying an image of something that you are not." (David Edmondson)

6

A Created King:

"So God created man in his own image, in the image of God created he him; male and female created he them."
Genesis 1:27

I have an awesome assignment in this life. That assignment given to me by God is to be a shepherd and minister to His people. Most of the time, my life is filled with blessings, love and peace, but every once in a while hard times come – just as in everyone's life who has lived, is living, or will live here in this world.

John 16: 33 reads, *"In this world you shall have tribulation but be of good cheer for I* (Jesus) *have overcome the world."*

Jesus gave us that truth to comfort us in times of hardship, to know He has promised victory.

In my times of trial, there are a few thoughts that I constantly focus on. One of those thoughts is who God says He has created me to be.

Let me stop here for just a moment and let you in on a little key that will help you make it to your created destiny. That key is: **Be careful what you look at**.

Now I am not speaking only of books or magazines. I am referring to what you allow your mind to envision and focus on. The mind is the battlefield where victory is won or lost.

Stock car drivers are told not to look at the outside wall of the track when they are racing. The reason is because whatever you focus on you will move toward. This is why **it is so important for us to know more about what God says about us and our lives, than we know about the circumstances and world around us**.

Lot's wife was only mentioned in two different passages of the Bible. The Bible doesn't give her name, age, lineage or hair color. One thing that we do read is in Genesis 19:26:

> *"But his* (Lot's) *wife looked back from behind him, and she became a pillar of salt."*

There is a very powerful truth that God is trying to show us in this passage. "Be very careful what you look at!"

We know that God had a plan for Lot's wife because He saved her from death. You must get this one thing through your head. **As long as there is breath in your body God has a plan for you to be used for His purpose**.

While striving to reach her destiny in life, Lot's wife lost focus on what was ahead and chose to look at her past, even though the Lord, speaking through His angels, warned them not to look back (v. 17). The Bible tells us that our past is "hidden" or "dead" in Christ. So when Lot's wife chose to look at her dead past she became what she focused on.

Jesus told us in Matthew 5:13 that we are the salt of the earth. Lot's wife had a God-created destiny to be used by God and affect people's lives for Him. But because of what she chose to look at, she "became" a useless pile of what she could have been. She didn't instantly turn into a pile of salt but with each step of misused focus she

8

became a stockpile of missed opportunities and forsaken destiny. You have the final choice in what you look at.

Paul told the Philippians, "*this one thing I do, forgetting those things which are behind, and reaching forth unto those things which are before, I press toward the mark for the prize of the high calling of God in Christ Jesus.*" (Philippians 3:13-14)

Choose wisely what you envision!

Let's get back to our image. I began to share about hard times and my assignment to shepherd God's people. I meet with people day after day who are mixed up in drugs, alcohol, adultery, fornication, gossip, doubt, worry and low self-esteem. You name it, people everywhere, of all shapes, sizes, colors and nationalities deal with sin and its price.

But I have found that there is one thing that can keep us in constant victory in this life. That one thing is for us to know who God has created us to be and why. The fact is, God has created me to be a king. If you know you were created to be the image of God you must know who God is.

Let's look at just a few scriptures from the Bible to help us determine who God is, so we will know what image we are created to be like.

In 1 Timothy 6:15, Jesus is described as "the blessed and only Potentate, the King of kings, and Lord of lords." In Revelation, the Lord is called "Lord of lords, and King of kings." Once again, in Revelation 19:16, concerning the return of our God, it is written, "And he hath on his vesture and on his thigh a name written, KING OF KINGS, AND LORD OF LORDS."

We have now established who Christ our Savior is. He is our God, our King, and we are created with His image and His likeness. This only leaves me with one question for you. What are you looking at?

When life says you are worthless, God says you are a king. When people call you a failure, Jesus calls you king. What you put in front of you will get in you. If I believe God created me in His image and His likeness, why can't I believe He sees me as who He is?

The word "image" depicts someone looking into a mirror and seeing himself. This is God's motive for creating you. So when He looks at you, He sees Himself.

This is liberating to a heart that can conceive the fact that God loves you so much He looks past your sins, faults and miscues to find who you really are: A KING – not because you deserve to be, but because He created you to be.

This is what you need to focus on. Do not allow yourself to be moved by feelings. Don't be swayed by emotions. And please don't become who people say you are, because their opinion of you will change daily. See yourself as God sees you. A King! Today is the day for you to see yourself as God created you – in His image! And, of course, we know what His character looks like: victorious, faithful, loving, kind, self confident, happy, full of joy and adorned with a king's robe and crown. He is sitting in His throne making sure everything works together for your good (Romans 8:28). What a wonderful God! And what an awesome image!

Remember 1 John 3:2 says,

"Beloved, now are we the sons of God, and it doth not yet appear what we shall be: but we know that, when he shall appear, we shall be like him; for we shall see him as he is."

"You don't drown by falling in the water; you drown by staying there." (Edwin Lewis Cole)

A Command to Produce:

"And God blessed them, and God said unto them, Be fruitful, and multiply, and replenish the earth..." Genesis 1:28

———

Have you ever wondered why God created you? I mean, let's get real, here. We are talking about the God of Heaven and Earth. He created all things, and all things exist because of Him. (Ephesians 3:9)

We look at all the beautiful things He has created and we stand in awe. We think of heaven, angels, landscapes and His glory; our minds cannot begin to imagine the endless pleasures God has created.

However, after seeing and hearing about all the spectacular things God has made, our lives with all of our faults and miscues cannot seem to compare to what we know God can do and has done. Our vision is fixed on the lackluster lives we seem to be stuck with. This is the mindset we live by: the fatal thought of "less than," because everything we see of our old selves and our old lives is less than the awesome beauty in Him and His kingdom.

It is this kind of short-sighted thinking that has kept so many people from experiencing greatness in this world.

Remember, what you put in front of you will get in you, and you will become what is in you.

Everything begins with a thought. When Adam and Eve were in the Garden of Eden, what was the beginning of their fall? Let's look at this account in Genesis 3:1-5.

"Now the serpent was more subtle than any beast of the field which the LORD God had made. And he said unto the woman, Yea, hath God said, Ye shall not eat of every tree of the garden? And the woman said unto the serpent, We may eat of the fruit of the trees of the garden: But of the fruit of the tree, which is in the midst of the garden, God hath said You shall not eat of it, neither shall you touch it, lest you die. And the serpent said unto the woman, You shall not surely die: For God does know that in the day you eat thereof, then your eyes shall be opened, and you shall be as gods, knowing good and evil."

The question was, what was the beginning of Adam and Eve's separation from God? The answer is: one wrong thought. See, the serpent (devil) knew if he could get Eve's mind off of the truth and get her to believing a lie, she would fall. Sin was formed from one thought. The Bible says in Isaiah 14:13 speaking of *Lucifer, "For thou has said in thine heart, I will ascend into heaven, I will exalt my throne above the stars of God."*

Even Lucifer became something he wasn't created to be. All because of one wrong thought he allowed into his heart. Satan knew that if he could get Eve to believe a lie, God's most prized creation would fall and become something God did not create them to be.

The mind is the battlefield!

The truth is found in Proverbs 23:7, *"For as he thinks in his heart so is he."*

What you say about yourself when no one is around is who you will become. Knowing this, let's take just a minute and see one thing God created us to do. When I know who God says I am, everything else must line up with that thought or it must go!

In Genesis 1:28, God commanded mankind to produce. He said to Adam and Eve *"Be fruitful and multiply."* I want to make a statement here that you may or may not like.

If your life is not productive, you are sinning against the creative power of God. He created mankind and commissioned us primarily to be productive. Productivity does not come by holding a remote, sitting in front of a TV screen. Nor does productivity come from those who have a "stinking thinking" problem.

Productive people don't wait for things to happen in their lives they get out and make things happen. That is the ability to produce.

God commands every one of us to produce in this life. The ability to produce begins with the ability to look forward and think the way God thinks. The way God thinks is, "If I don't have it, I will create it." Everything God created began with one thought. After God thought it, He had the power within Himself to produce it.

Remember whose image and likeness you were created in? That is right; God's image and likeness. Do not let any person, place, thing or thought stop you from doing what God commanded you to do. God has commanded you to produce.

The worst question that could be asked by someone at a funeral service is, "What could have been?" Have you ever thought about what your life could have been *if...* ?

We have all thought this at least once.

Let me tell you something that is stinking thinking. I heard a great man of God tell a story one time about him and his mother. As a boy, he and his mother were at a store and they bought a certain item. After buying the item they began to walk home. On their way home, he saw the item they had just purchased in the window of another store and said to his mother, "Lets go see if the item is cheaper in this store."

When the mother heard her son make this statement, she replied "Son, once you make a decision, never look back."

That will set you free if you will let it.

One of my favorite scriptures is found in 2 Corinthians 5:17. It says, *"Therefore if any man be in Christ, he is a new creature: old things are passed away; behold, all things are become new."*

This thought will keep you in a state of productivity. Yesterday's miscues bring knowledge, but today's light presents a fresh start! Begin today making your life fulfill what God commanded you to do: PRODUCE!

"Don't consume your tomorrows feeding on your yesterdays." (John L. Mason)

Taking Back Control:

"...and replenish the earth, and subdue it: and have dominion over the fish of the sea, and over the fowl of the air, and over every living thing that moves upon the earth." Genesis 1:28

———

"Well if it be God's will, it will happen."

I know you have heard or maybe even said this statement one time or a hundred other times before. This is one of the devil's greatest masterpieces. Through this statement the enemy cancels one of the commands of God to mankind: to subdue the earth and everything on it.

The word "subdue" means to conquer, bring into bondage, force, keep under, or to bring into subjection. God started off by commanding us to take control of our lives and everything around us. We do an okay job of subduing or taking control of animals, landscapes, and even other people, but when it comes to taking control of our own lives guess what we say? "If it be God's will, it will happen." This is simply a cop-out to your creative instinct of taking control.

God allows Himself to be limited by two things. One of the things God allows Himself to be limited to is His Word. God will do everything He has said He will do in the Bible. The Bible is truth. It is the infallible Word of the living God. What the Bible says about God, what He will do, and everything He has promised us is true. We must understand that God is God, and beside Him there is no other (Mark 12:32). He can do whatever He wants at any moment He wants. As believers like to say, He is sovereign, But He allows Himself to be limited to do what He has already promised in the Bible.

The second thing God allows Himself to be limited by is man's will.

By *man's* will?

Absolutely!

See, when God created mankind, the thing that separates us from all other creations is the fact that we have our own will to consider when making choices. For instance, when God first created Adam, the Bible states that God brought all the animals to Adam and God asked Adam what he wanted to call each of the animals. This shows the power of choice or will God created man with.

Sin entered into mankind because Adam chose the gift (Eve) over the giver (God). He opted for his own will instead of what God declared was His will – that is, to not eat of the fruit of the tree of knowledge of good and evil.

See, Eve was tricked by a rewording of something God has said. But Adam knew that if he ate of the fruit of the tree of knowledge of good and evil, he would be separated from the Spirit of the Lord forever. Because of man's free will to choose, Adam willed himself to choose Eve instead of God. So his destiny was changed forever.

Was it God's will for this to happen? Or was it man's will? Couldn't God have somehow intervened or caused something to happen so Adam would not have sinned? Yes, God could have done anything. He is God.

Well, the question then would arise, "Why didn't He do something?"

Because God had already made a decision long ago when he created man in His image and likeness with the ability to choose. God wants to be chosen, not to force or trick people into choosing Him! This desire of God is the foundation of all creation. Everything was created for God's pleasure and God gets no greater pleasure than when one of His creations choose Him and His ways over everything else.

What I have just created for you through the truth of the Word of God is a problem. The problem is, you can no longer blame God for your laziness and misfortunes. So what are you going to do now?

I have an answer: Subdue!

Take control of your life and don't let other people and their ignorance stop you from greatness.

The Word of God in Deuteronomy 30:19 says,

"I have set before you life and death, blessing and cursing: therefore choose life, that both thou and thy seed may live."

The Lord said in Isaiah 45:2,

"I will go before thee, and make the crooked places straight: I will break in pieces the gates of brass, and cut in sunders the bars of iron."

You have no excuse if you fail to make something out of your life. God has created you to succeed. All Heaven is cheering you on, and your past has been forgotten.

What is stopping you?

What does Romans 8:31 & 32 say?

"What shall we then say to these things? If God be for us, who can be against us? He that spared not his own Son, but delivered him up for us all, how shall he not with him also freely give us all things?"

"To achieve your dreams, you must embrace adversity and make failure a regular part of your life. If you're not

failing, you're probably not really moving forward."
(John Maxwell)

Made to Reign:

"…and have dominion over the fish of the sea, and over the fowl of the air, and over every living thing that moveth upon the earth." Genesis 1:28

———

What does it mean when God commanded mankind to have dominion over everything He created?

First let's look at the word "have." When the Bible tells us that God told man to "have" dominion, it means that dominion was a gift. This means God gave man a gift.

You don't have to work for this dominion or act a certain way to obtain it. It was a gift from God to His creation, and the Bible states in Romans 11:29, *"For the gifts and calling of God are without repentance."*

This lets me know that God does not give you something or call you for a purpose and then take it from you when you mess up or don't perform well. I don't know about you, but understanding that truth alone has set me free from a lot of fear and condemnation.

So the gift God gave to man at the beginning, He has not taken from man now. This means God did not ask me to have dominion, nor did He suggest I pursue dominion. The text proclaims that God **gave** us dominion!

We must then ask ourselves the question, What is this gift of "dominion" that God has given us? The word dominion means "to prevail against, reign, make to rule, or take over." God has given mankind the gift of reigning. That's what a king does, isn't it?

This statement is palatable to religious minds because we know that in the sweet by and by; way up in heaven, we shall reign with God. But we are not dealing with heaven in this scripture. Notice that the verse cited above says "*...dominion...upon the earth.*" Man and woman were created and placed on this earth. This is where they received the gift of reigning. God has made me to reign on this earth, at this time in history, not because I deserve it but because it was a gift from my Father.

This is what you must remind yourself of in order to overcome all the negative thoughts that will try to keep you under service to this world and its way of operation.

It is in our creative make-up to reign. Romans 3:4 makes a bold statement about the trustworthiness of the Word of God, "*Let God be true, but every man a liar; as it is written, That thou mightest be justified in thy sayings, and mightest overcome when thou art judged.*"

In the book of Romans, the Apostle Paul is dealing with Christians trying to serve God while the world is telling them they have to live by the law. Paul deals with things like circumcision, faith, judgment, and the promise of God. When reading this book you can sense Paul's frustration in dealing with what the world wants Christians to believe and what God has done in and for us.

Finally he makes this statement to the children of God. Let what God has said be the truth and everything man says be considered a lie if it doesn't line up. He goes on to say if you believe the Word of God you will be justified by it and you will be made to overcome by its truth.

It isn't our job as Christians to prove the Word of God to be true, except as we live it out in our daily actions. God never asks us to prove His Word to be true and convince others that what He said was true. Don't get caught up in trying to prove what you believe. All God asks us to do is believe what He has said in His Word and the Word of God will prove itself. You will never be able to reign in this world as God has gifted you to do if you get caught up in what the world – and even a lot of Christians – believe.

It is easier to blame God and His supposed lack of equipping us to do what He asks us to do than to throw down all of our crutches and fight for what God has freely given us and asked us to do.

Which one will you be, the walking wounded assisted by faithless crutches, guided by worldly views of Heavenly promises, rationalizing with the mentality of a victim? Or will you be the reigning child of God? One who needs no other assistance than that of the Word of his or her Father? One who is led by the voice of God's Spirit and thinks as God thinks.

Whichever you decide to become, I pray that this statement will find you wherever you go: "You were made to Reign!"

Revelation 1:5&6 says,

"And from Jesus Christ, who is the faithful witness, and the first begotten of the dead, and the prince of the kings of the earth. Unto him that loved us, and washed us from our sins in his own blood. And hath made us kings and priests unto God and his Father; to him be glory and dominion forever and ever. Amen."

"Ninety-nine percent of failures come from people who have a habit of making excuses." (George Washington)

Living with a Mess:

"And the LORD God formed man of the dust of the ground..." Genesis 2:7

Have you ever felt like you were trying to make a dream house out of a dirt pile? I mean, have you ever felt like you have made such a mess out of your life at times that you think you should just give up on your dreams?

Let me tell you something: you are at a great place in your life. God specializes in creating greatness out of dirt.

Listen how the Bible refers to God in Isaiah 64:8:

"But now, O LORD, thou art our father; we are the clay, and thou our potter; and we all are the work of thy hand."

Sometimes you are going to feel like dirt. That is okay because to be honest, that is what your body is made from. God created us from dirt and to dirt we shall return. Though my flesh is dirt and that is what I am, dirt is not *who* I am.

You can see in the second chapter of Genesis why you have to distinguish between what is the flesh and who is the real you.

23

"And the LORD God formed man of the dust of the ground, and breathed into his nostrils the breath of life; and man became a living soul." Genesis 2:7

Your flesh was created from dirt and will always at times resemble what it is, but who you are is established on the image and likeness of God, breathed into you by God. Who you are is not based on what God used to create your body. Your flesh will lie to you, because it wants to be in control. And if you listen to this lie you will become this lie.

The lie of our flesh is this: *what* we are is ultimately *who* we are. That is not true.

Let me explain.

I am not what you see when I am in your company. The Bible clearly explains that we as humans consist of three parts. We are spirits, we have a soul, and we live in a body. The fact is, who I am never has and never will change into the image of what I am. I am a spirit created by the breath of God in His likeness with His image. That will never change! That is who I am!

My soul which consists of my mind, will, and emotions, is the part of me that fights against the inner me – who I really am. My spirit is never depressed, out of touch, sad, or moody. My soul, on the other hand, may be happy one minute and sad the next. That is why one day you may feel good about yourself and the very next day you feel worthless. It is because your mind, will and emotions are affected by the world around you.

If you do not identify the difference between your spirit (who you are) and your soul (what you are), you will live in constant torment. You body is your fleshly shell that operates and is directed by your soul. Some people like to separate the soul and the body but I have found that they work together. The Bible says that the flesh (body) and the soul (mind, will and emotions) are both enemies of God (Romans 7:18 & 8:7).

The fact of the matter is we are all "living with a mess." Everyone at times feels the symptoms of who we are being tormented by what we are. Have you ever felt like you were out of place, like you just didn't fit in? This should be normal for Christians. We should feel different and even like we don't belong. That's because we don't belong here. We are citizens of heaven, the Bible says. ("*For our conversation is in heaven; from whence also we look for the Savior, the Lord Jesus Christ.*" Philippians 3:20 "Conversation" means citizenship.)

We cannot live out of the conditions facing what we are; we must rather live out of the position that has been set in place because of who we are.

Our conditions in this life change everyday. One day you may feel good about yourself and those around you. You may think you can touch the stars and accomplish anything set before you. Then one day, one week, or even one month later you may hate yourself. You may feel worthless, lost, hopeless and lonely. What has changed? Who you are? No! The only thing that has changed is the conditions surrounding your body and soul.

When your conditions change, your fleshly soul and body immediately begin to try to line up with the conditions surrounding you. What you are, what you look like, and sometimes even what you believe, fall into the trap that "what you are is based on what you are surrounded by." This is not the lifestyle God wants His children to live.

The Bible declares in 1 Timothy 6:12, "*Fight the good fight of faith…*"

What does the Apostle Paul mean by "fighting the good fight of faith"? The fight of faith Paul is talking about in this verse is dealing with the fight between who you are and what you are.

25

Let's take this thought a little deeper as I try to explain what is referred to as "the mystery."

When someone gets born again and asks Jesus to come into their lives and to be their Lord and Savior, who they are changes. In 2 Corinthians 5:17, the Bible states, *"Therefore if any man be in Christ, he is a new creature: old things are passed away; behold, all things are become new."*

Well, we know that when we got saved our body didn't change. We also know that, for the most part, our mind, will and emotions stayed the same. So what passed away and what became new? Was it what we are that changed or who we are? We have established that, essentially, what we are did not change. So it must be that who we are changed.

Who you were changed immediately when you asked Jesus to come into your life. You went from being a servant of the world to a Son of God. The conditions surrounding you didn't change, but the position of who you were did. The fight that we are in everyday – the "fight of faith" as Paul describes it – is the war between who you are and what you are. You are God's child (Romans 8:16)! You are God's friend (Luke 12:4)! Your life is hidden in the life of Christ (Colossians 3:3)! You are seated in Christ, at the Father's right hand (Ephesians 2:6)! These things describe who you are. Though what you are may not look, act, feel or even believe who you are, that does not negate the fact that **you are who God says you are!!!**

The battle to believe who you are according to the Word of God, instead of what your circumstances say you are, is the "Fight of Faith." It isn't really much of a fight when you realize all that matters is who God says you are.

I challenge you to search God's Word for who He says you are. There is not a dream you can't achieve if you know who you are. You will no longer be swayed by the opinions of people, the voice of the enemy, nor the circumstances of the world when you KNOW who you are. When you begin to live out of your position and refuse to live by your conditions, you can live with a mess and still live in victory!

Look at what the prodigal son did in Luke 15. He had left family, friends, wealth, and comfort for a life of pleasure and recklessness. He chose to leave the palace and ended up dining with pigs. His condition had certainly changed. The man had lost everything and had no way of getting it back. While fighting swine for food to survive, the Bible says, "He came to himself" and said, *"How many hired servants of my father's have bread enough and to spare, and I perish with hunger! I will arise and go to my father..."* When the Bible states that the man "came to himself," it means the man remembered who he was. He didn't look at his conditions or what he had done. He remembered who he was through his father.

As the story continues, when the man got home his father threw a big party and the man received everything he once had. This is what God is offering you.

What you are, and the conditions of this world that are surrounding you will keep you in the pig pin. But if you can just gain the knowledge of who you are in your Father, you will realize there is nothing that has not been freely given for you.

Living with a mess does not have to mean you are a mess!

Who does God say you are? Ephesians 2:14:

"For he is our peace, who hath made both one, and hath broken down the middle wall of partition between us."

"God does not patch up the old life, or make certain repairs on the life: He gives a new life, through the new birth." (Unknown)

Receiving His Breath:

"...and breathed into his nostrils the breath of life; and man became a living soul." Genesis 2:7

———

My prayer is that the words that fill the pages of this section will fill you with peace, purpose, hope, and God's love.

As you begin to read this section, I am praying and believing that God will breathe a fresh breath of His presence into you. I feel everyone that picks up this book will encounter a new level of the glory of God.

Right now, take a minute and ask God to breathe a fresh breath of His presence on you. After you ask Him, begin to thank Him and just take a deep breath in and receive from your Father a fresh strength and peace in His love. That's it, let God fill you with the kisses of His lips! After taking a minute to enjoy your Best Friend and Father, we will continue on into our study.

What you have just experienced was the breath of God that is with you, inside you and around you every moment of your life (Ephesians 4:6).

One of the greatest misconceptions Christians have is the thought of needing a preacher, church or feeling to get into the presence of God.

Let me ask you a question. How many times did God command light to shine in the darkness? God only commanded light to shine one time, right? See, God creates and has created everything by a simple command of His voice. One day, God looked over the balcony of Heaven into an abyss of nothing, and out of nothing He created everything with one simple breath. There was no Earth, no trees, no animals, no stars and no life. If you or I had been standing in Heaven looking into blackness we would have said there is no hope out there and turned around and sang hymns with the angels. Thank God, He isn't like us! Thank God that He can look into nothing and see something no one else can see – kind of like your life before you met Jesus. Or maybe that is the way your life looks right now: dark, void, and without any hope or form.

My friend, don't lose hope. If you will listen, you can hear the breath of God and His creative words – "Let there be light!" – echoing into your dark life.

The fact is, all you need to do is receive the breath of God that already fills your being. God spoke only one time thousands of years ago and light was created. That light has never ceased to exist and perform because it was created by God's eternal breath. Your Bible states very clearly that in the first stages of human existence, God breathed into man and, with the same breath that created an eternal light, man became "a living soul." The wonderful thing about this statement is that because we were created by one blast of God's breath, the same breath that made us live has never ceased to dwell within us.

Meditate on that truth.

So, my friends, when you need a touch from God or when you long to be renewed by His Spirit, just "breathe." The Spirit of the living God is alive in you. In fact, you are alive because of His creative breath continuing to resound those remarkable words, "let there be...," in your being.

Let me explain just what it means to have the Spirit of God living in you. (Hold on to your hair because this could get a little exciting!) Let's begin in the beginning.

Before we do, it is very important to keep in mind what we are ultimately trying to get an understanding about, and that is "the breath of God." We know and read in the Bible that God "is one God" (1 Timothy 2:5), and "beside Him there is no other." (Isaiah 44:6) We also read about the trinity consisting of God the Father, Jesus the Son, and the Holy Spirit ("For there are three that bear record in heaven, the Father, the Word, and the Holy Ghost: and these three are one." – 1 John 5: 7)

To understand how the Spirit of God, through the blood of Jesus, can at all times live within the heart of a sinful man by the grace of God, we must know how They can be Three while at the same time existing as One. (That was a mouthful!)

I would like to explain this to you the way my mother explained it to me years ago. Imagine an egg. (Yes an egg. Now don't get mad at my illustration, I am not saying God is an egg. Just go with me, and in the end I promise you will see the simple analogy.) While thinking of an egg, we know that the egg consists of three distinct parts. First, you have the outer part called the "shell." Once you break open the shell you will see a clear runny substance we call the egg "white." (I don't know how we came up with that name, do you?) Then in the middle of this white substance there is the yellow part of the egg or the "yolk." Three separate and distinct parts exist in one simple egg. Similarly, you have one God who exists in three forms.

Let's go a little deeper and try to catch this rabbit.

We see the first distinction between God and the Lord God (Jesus) while reading of the creation of all things.

When God spoke, the Bible indicates that the Lord God (the Word) came out of Him and performed what God had said (Genesis 2). You may think, David, you are grasping at straws now. Please just stay with me. Keep your mind and heart open as the Spirit of God reveals Himself to us in a deeper and sounder way.

An interesting change occurs between verses 2 and 3 in Genesis chapter 2. Look at those verses together:

"And God blessed the seventh day, and sanctified it: because that in it he had rested from all his work which God created and made.

"These are the generations of the heavens and of the earth when they were created, in the day that the LORD God made the earth and the heavens..."

In verse 2, God is referred to as "the LORD God," (Hebrew: *Jehovah Elohim*) whereas, in every prior reference, He is called "God" (Hebrew: *Elohim*). In the notes of the 1917 edition of the *Scofield Reference Bible*, Cyrus Scofield points out, "It is significant that the first appearance of the name Jehovah in Scripture follows the creation of man. It was God (*Elohim*) who said, 'Let us make man in our image' (Genesis 1:26); but when man, as in the second chapter of Genesis, is to fill the scene and become dominant over creation, it is the Lord God (*Jehovah Elohim*) who acts. This clearly indicates a special relation of Deity, in His Jehovah character, to man, and all Scripture emphasizes this."

I can correctly state that there is a distinction between God (The Father) and the Lord God (Jesus) because of many scriptures, but for the sake of time I will just give you a few.

Romans 10:9: *"That if thou shalt confess with thy mouth the Lord Jesus, and shalt believe in thine heart that God hath raised him from the dead, thou shalt be saved."*
(Paul calls Jesus "Lord Jesus.")

1 Timothy 6:14&15: *"...that thou keep this commandment without spot, unrebukeable, until the appearing of our Lord Jesus Christ: Which in his times he shall show, who is the blessed and only Potentate, the King of kings, and Lord of lords."* (Here, Jesus is referred to as the "Lord of Lords.")

Revelation 17:14: *"These shall make war with the Lamb, and the Lamb shall overcome them: for he is Lord of lords, and King of kings: and they that are with him are called, and chosen, and faithful."* (Here again, the Bible specifically calls Jesus the "Lord of Lords.")

Revelation 19:16: *"And he hath on his vesture and on his thigh a name written, KING OF KINGS, AND LORD OF LORDS."* (Once again, we see Jesus described as "Lord of Lords.")

What I would like for you to understand is that God the Father has never, will never, and doesn't need to ever leave His throne created for Him and by Him in Heaven. At the same time, when God spoke, part of Him – His Breath, the Lord, the Word – created what God said.
We also read that it was "the Lord God" that fellowshipped with Adam while he was in the garden

(Genesis 3). It was the Lord God that literally created all things, walked the Earth, talked with the prophets, and eventually came in to the borrowed womb of a virgin girl named Mary. This is why Jesus could say to His disciples in John 14:9, "*he that hath seen me hath seen the Father.*"

While also saying in Matthew 12:50, "*For whosoever shall do the will of my Father which is in heaven, the same is my brother, and sister, and mother,*" Jesus shows the distinction between Himself and the Father.

Again in 1 Corinthians 8:6, we see that everything is created "of" God and "by" Jesus: "*But to us there is but one God, the Father, **of whom are all things** and we in him; and one Lord Jesus Christ, **by whom are all things** and we by him.*" (Emphasis added to scripture reference)

Now that we have made a distinction between God the Father and the Lord Jesus, let's go into the third part of the trinity and get back to receiving His breath.

I have tried in a very short period of time to show you how God spoke and the Lord God, or Jesus, performed. Soon after the Lord created man, we know that man chose to disobey God, and sin came into mankind. Because of this sin, death or separation existed between a sinless God and His sinful creation. God, in all of His wisdom, created a plan to save and reunite Himself with His creation so they could once again fellowship forever in unity. This "plan of salvation" would call on the Lord God Himself to come to Earth, be born of flesh, live a sinless life, be crucified, buried and raised from the dead, after which He would present Himself to the Father as the sacrifice for all sin.

The Lord God, Jesus, came to the Earth and was born of a virgin. Now we have the Father God in Heaven and the Lord God, Jesus, here on Earth in the form of a man. Now let's see how we get the Holy Spirit into the mix.

Let's look at John 14:16-18, where Jesus says:

"And *I will pray the Father,* and *he shall give you another Comforter,* that he may abide with you for ever; Even the Spirit of truth; whom the world cannot receive, because it seeth him not, neither knoweth him: but ye know him; for *he dwelleth with you, and shall be in you I* will not leave you comfortless: *I will come to you*" (Emphasis added to scripture reference)

A few things I would like for you to remember from this scripture as we continue. Jesus is about to die for the sins of all mankind when He tells His disciples:

#1. "I will pray to the Father and He will send you another Comforter."

#2. This Spirit will abide and live in Christians forever.

#3. Jesus then says: "I won't leave you comfortless. I will come to you."

Imagine a natural father who has been the comforting provider for his children, and he is about to step outside the house in a storm. The children see him leaving and, as children might, they start to get worried he might be leaving them for good. He stops at the door and says, Don't worry. I'm not leaving you alone. I'm coming back to you in a few minutes. That's a rough analogy of what Jesus is telling His disciples. "Don't worry. I'm coming back." But the interesting thing is that He says it in the context of speaking about the Holy Spirit, the Comforter (vv. 16-17). That indicates the Holy Spirit to come is His (Jesus') Spirit, or the Spirit of Christ.

In fact, Peter refers to the Holy Spirit as the Spirit of Christ, in 1 Peter 1:11 ("*Searching what, or what manner of time the Spirit of Christ which was in them did signify, when it testified beforehand the sufferings of Christ, and the glory that should follow.*"), as does Paul in Romans 8:9 ("*But ye are not in the flesh, but in the Spirit, if so be that the Spirit of God dwell in you. Now if any man have not the Spirit of Christ, he is none of his.*")

35

Let's now look at Luke's depiction of the Jesus' very last moments on the cross, in verses 23:46: *"And when Jesus had cried with a loud voice, he said, Father, into thy hands I commend my spirit: and having said thus, he gave up the ghost."* Here, Jesus is on the cross about to die and He cries out to the Father, "Into *thy hands* I give you *my* Spirit..."

Now after all of this you have got to be asking yourself what in the world I'm trying to say. Or maybe you are thinking, what does this entire study have to do with my purpose and God's breath?

It is vitally important for you to understand that God's breath in your life is far more than a feeling. We all know feelings come and go, all the while changing in any given moment.

The "breath" of God once created all things through the person of the Lord God Jesus Christ. After creation, the breath of God in the person of the Lord Jesus Christ became flesh and died for our sins. While the smoke cleared from the battle between sin and the Savior, the breath of God that once created everything through the person of the Lord Jesus Christ was given to live inside of us in the gift of the Holy Spirit.

That is how I can say to you, if you need to be refreshed by the Spirit of God, you should look no further than He that lives on the inside of you. The Holy Spirit, the Spirit of God, the Spirit of the Lord, the Spirit of Jesus – whatever you want to call Him – He exists by one simple "breath." This breath that God breathed into the first man, Adam, is the same breath that was breathed into you by the second "Adam," the Lord Jesus Christ – our Savior, friend, Lord, companion, and our "Breath."

By one breath, breathed into a lifeless dirt carcass by a living powerful God, came each and every one of us. The same breath of God that filled you when you were in the womb of your mother cleansed you when you asked for forgiveness. It is the same Spirit you sense while at church, praying with your pastor, or struggling to make it through a tough day.

The breath of God forever lives in you because of the grace of God, through the blood of Jesus, as the person of the Holy Spirit. God wants you now to receive a fresh breath that comes from a fresh revelation.

Receive His Breath!

"By God's breath I became, by His breath I am, and by His breath I shall be. What else does a person need, save the Breath of God?" (David Edmondson)

You Need Help:

"And the LORD God said, It is not good that the man should be alone..." Genesis. 2:18

"I need help!"

This is a cry that scares us and even, at times, restricts us from being successful. We humans – and especially men – think that when we acknowledge that there are times we need help we are showing weakness. We are trained from an early age to do everything ourselves and never admit when we are not strong or wise enough to accomplish a task.

"Help" is a word for cowards, weaklings or someone who is drowning. Only weak, stupid, unfocused or lazy people need help. Isn't this what you have been trained to think? The idea of needing someone's help is an admission of failure and lack, right?

I would like to share something with you that will save you a lot of headache and loneliness. If you have been alive for more than thirty seconds in this world you will need someone's help sometime or another. It doesn't matter how educated, strong, manly, wise or cunning you are; you need people to help you at times.

Let's take a few moments and evaluate our scripture reference for today:

"It is not good that the man should be alone..."
Genesis. 2:18

God created man with His image and likeness. But while man was like God in that he was a three-part being – body, soul and spirit – he had no one in *his* own image with whom to commune. Since Adam, by himself, could not procreate; he would have no companion and no children – no one like himself to fellowship with. God had created man for communion with Himself, and immediately the compassion of the Father wanted His created son Adam to have communion with others in his own likeness.

This word "alone" will reveal to us the way Adam existed for a span of time in which he was so much like God, to exist as man there had to be a change in Adam's make up.

The word "alone" may be broken down to mean "all one." Adam, being created with God's image, in God's likeness, existed as one perfect being. As God is all one in Himself and He needs no other to exist; Adam was created to exist as God, as one perfect being. Yet, just as God wanted more communion, He knew man would want more communion.

You may be asking yourself, What did Adam look like, or how long did he exist this way? These are questions that I cannot answer, but Adam gave all the animals names and had dominion for a period of time "all-one." This was the created stage where God said, It is not good for man to be alone, or all one.

Thus, because mankind was all one in himself, God said, I will cause a separation in the created man and form out of him a separate being to hold Adam through life. So God formed woman.

Again, we can see that the first man, Adam, was so much like God that when God wanted to create a helpmate for Adam, He did not reach into the dust of the Earth, but he pulled from Adam what was already existing in him to begin with.

As a born-again believer in Jesus Christ, everything you need to be successful is already in you. God created you with every talent, ability and the equipment you need to accomplish your dreams. And anything else not resident in you, He gave through the knowledge of Himself. Peter said, *"his divine power hath given unto us all things that pertain unto life and godliness, through the knowledge of him that hath called us to glory and virtue."* (2 Peter 1:3)

You just need to "lie down" and let the infallible hand of God remove from you the help you need!

See, the Bible states that God caused Adam to lie down and sleep. Peter said it like this in 1Peter 5:7, *"Casting all your care upon him (Jesus); for he cares for you."*

I would like to take just a second and speak to your spirit and let you know you were not created to carry the cares of this life. The Spirit of God says to cast or throw your cares as far away from you as you can. God will then take what you have thrown to Him and He will supply the need to fulfill the care.

We were created to be the *"head and not the tail, above only and never beneath,"* according to Deuteronomy 28:13. You can't be above in this world if you are being pulled down by the pressures and cares of this life. Throw it to the Lord. Don't lay it down because you will trip over it and eventually pick it back up. Throw it as far from you as it takes for your heart and mind to release it.

This is why the woman with the alabaster box of ointment broke the vessel over the feet of the Lord. The breaking of the vessel signified that what she was carrying was no longer worth the price that she had to pay to keep it.

I heard one man say, what you open you can close again. She didn't just open the box; she broke it, so the opportunity to close it up and take it with her did not exist.

Throw it, break it, cast it or release it; whatever you have to do to give your cares to God, do it and live.

Back to Adam and the need for help.

God reached into Adam and formed woman from man. Imagine what a shocking sight it was when Adam woke up. His first words were, *"This is flesh of my flesh and bone of my bone."* Adam's amazement was, "This is me sitting beside me."

You would not believe what you will look like in a year if you lie down and allow God to excavate you out of you. The fact is you don't know what is in you. That is why God allows you to have "desires." Desire is nothing more than the you inside of you trying to let you know what is in you. (You might want to read that again.) Later in this study I will elaborate more on this issue.

It is recorded in Psalms 37:4, *"God will give you the desires of your heart."* This doesn't mean God is like Santa Clause with all the goodies you can think of. What it does mean is God puts desires in you and then, because He is so good, He turns around and fulfills them. (No, you know I'm not talking about the superficial, counterfeit desires your flesh has acquired. I'm talking about the genuine, holy desires for communion and to glorify Him by your actions, and your soul's innermost desires for peace, love, joy and all the other fruit of the Spirit.)

This creating and fulfilling of a desire is what God did for Adam. God saw that even though Adam was in a

42

perfect state of being, even though he had all knowledge, strength, courage and dominion, it was not good. Mankind needed help. Adam needed someone to help him make decisions, hold him, talk with him and play with him. It was not good, God said, for man to try and live with out someone to help him.

My question for you is, if Adam – who lived in a perfect world, had a perfect body and complete, unhindered communication with God – needed help, what makes you any different? You need to realize "help" is not a bad thing. As a matter of fact "help" is what made God look at mankind and say, "Now this is very good."

Proverbs 11:14 *"Where no counsel is, the people fall: but in the multitude of counselors there is safety."*

"Desire is the sensation to push, because your dream is ready to be born." (David Edmondson)

Someone Needs You:

"...I will make him an help meet for him." Genesis 2:18

———

One great, often-overlooked thing about God is that He is a God of preparation.

For the sake of discussion, let's look at our fleshly body for a moment.

According to the Word of God, He never intended for mankind to get sick. Let me explain how I can make this statement. We know that sickness is an effect, a result, of sin. Now, I am not saying if you are sick in your body you are living in sin. What I am saying, is that sickness did not exist until man sinned in the Garden of Eden. The Bible states in Romans 6:23, *"For the wages of sin is death*; but the gift of God is eternal life through Jesus Christ our Lord."*

Sickness is in a cause-and-effect relationship with sin. Sin is the cause and sickness is the effect. We live in a hostile environment, one where sin has had reign for thousands of years, so that, to the soul that wants to live for God, living in a sinful world is like a human trying to live on the moon; that human would need to bring his own native environment with him in order to survive. To complete the analogy for you, faith in God's Word is the

45

equivalent of a space suit that brings the Kingdom of God's environment to Earth. It allows you to survive and thrive in this hostile environment of sin.

If sin did not exist, the effect of sin would not exist. Sickness is simply the dysfunction or death, if you will, of your physical body. Therefore, sickness is a wage or a price of sin. Not just personal sin, but also as a condition of living in a fallen world.

Adam was not created in sin, nor was he living in a world of sin. Sin entered into mankind *after* God created man. There is no sin in God, so there is no effect of sin in Him, which, in part, is sickness. Thus, man, being created in God's image, was created whole and completely well. That's the reason I can say God did not create man to be sick at any time. But God created mankind from the ground with an immune system, which is the natural instinct of your body to fight off sickness.

Why did God create us with an immune system if His will was for us to never be sick? He is a God of preparation.

Nothing sneaks up on God. That is why God is not moved by your circumstances. That's right, I said it. Your trials and the storms of your life do not make God react in any way. You may be asking yourself how can this be? God doesn't care about what I am going through?

Don't misunderstand. God cares about what you are going through. He cares so much that He has already made a way for you to escape (1Corinthians 10:13). Take the account in Mark chapter four. The Bible states that Jesus and His disciples were on a ship in the middle of a lake when a great storm arose. All the disciples were frantic and upset, but Jesus was in the bottom of the boat sleeping. (Now, don't make fun of them; we get bent all out of shape when storms arise in our lives and Jesus is there with us, also.) This shows us that God is not moved by our storms. Do you think for a minute that Jesus didn't know a storm was going to arise?

John 16:33 states, *"In this world, you shall have tribulation, but be of good cheer for I* [Christ] *have overcome the world."* The reason God is not moved by your storms or the trials you will face in your life is because He has already taken care of them. God did not only overcome or conquer your tribulations, the Bible says Jesus overcame the thing that produced your tribulation (The World!). This is why, when God takes care of a situation, it is over for good. Because He is such a God of preparation, it wasn't good enough to handle the tribulation alone. God went ahead and took control of the thing that caused the tribulation in the first place.

Notice Jesus didn't get up and rebuke the waves of the sea. Jesus rebuked the wind. Why did He rebuke the wind when it was the waves that were causing the damage?

Remember God is always prepared. He knew that what they *could* see wasn't the problem; it was what they *couldn't* see. The waves were tossing the boat, but the winds were directing the waves.

If you get only one thing from this study today, let it be this: God is at work on your behalf before you ever even see the effects of the storm. And the first time you ask for His help, God begins to speak His peace. Don't look at the effect of the storm and be fooled into thinking God isn't at work on your behalf. Just remember, God is rebuking the wind and it will not be long until the waves settle down again. He is always prepared!

This is the truth we see in the creation of man and woman. God knew that we would need help in some way at some time in our lives. Thus, He created people to help us. But the truth is, if we are going to find help from someone in our life, someone must be willing to help. God created in all of mankind the voice, or a sensation, that moves us with compassion. It prepares us to help

47

those around us who are in need. If you refuse to help someone in need, you are sinning against the creative power of God. Read what John had to say about those in need in 1John 3:17&18:

> *"But who ever hath this world's good, and seeth his brother have need, and shutteth up his bowels of compassion from him, how dwelleth the love of God in him? My little children, let us not love in word, neither in tongue; but in deed and in truth."*

The God of preparation has created each of us with an inward voice of compassion to be a help to those in need. You may be an answer to someone's prayers, but if you shut up the voice of compassion inside you, someone may go lacking. God may be prompting you to give financially to someone or to some church. Listen to your creative nature and be that help. You may be sensing the need to befriend someone, to fill a ministry gap at your church, or maybe even adopt a child. Be the voice that rebukes the wind that has caused stormy waves in someone else's life.

I know what you are thinking; "What is it going to cost me to help someone in need?"

The truth is, the cost of being that help is nothing compared to the wages you will reap by refusing to submit to the creative voice of God. The fact is, it will cost you something to help someone who is in need. It may cost you money, time, emotions, heartache, and maybe even your life. No words could bring closure to this thought any better than those spoken by Jesus himself when he said, *"For what shall it profit a man, if he shall gain the whole world, and lose his own soul?"* (Mark 8:36).

We get gun shy when it comes to helping people because of the price we have had to pay in the past. Prices like giving someone money to buy their children some food, but they spend it on cigarettes and alcohol. Or maybe you have taken your time to help someone in need, but when you called for help he or she was too busy and unwilling to make the sacrifice you made for them. Or probably the biggest one is the story we all know too well. You know the one, where you pour out your life to help a hurting person, you share your emotions, you give them a place in your heart, and even after all of this, they talk about you, they run you over with their words and leave you alone, broken, and in need of help yourself. These are the kinds of things that keep us from really helping other people.

I would love to say these things will not happen anymore, but the likelihood of one or more of these happening to you outweigh the chance that they won't. So it all comes down to what God has created us to do, and if I help others with the right heart motive, then even if they misuse my trust and help, I will not be shaken. See, God wants us to help people who are in need, but we must understand the difference between giving and becoming. See, I can give help to someone, but if they misuse my help, the only one affected is them.

But here's where we go wrong: we *become* the help we are trying to give. In other words we give expecting something in return. This is very dangerous, because if we don't receive the response we were expecting, our feelings get hurt. So the next time we are moved to help, those old feelings arise and we react out of selfishness instead of reacting from our creative voice of compassion.

So what you must do is give help to those who are in need expecting nothing in return. After you have given your help, turn and walk away. Do not become something you're not. You are just the conduit through which God chooses to flow. Conduit is nothing more than a plastic piece of pipe, but with the right wires on the inside and a good connection to the power source, it makes for an incredible piece of hardware. And remember, no structure is safe and well assembled without good conduit.

"When you know people's value, you can add value to them." (Unknown)

God Honors Your Input:

"And out of the ground the LORD God formed every beast of the field, and every fowl of the air; and brought them unto Adam to see what he would call them: and whatsoever Adam called every living creature, that was the name thereof." Genesis 2:19

———

I think that one greatly condemning thought that many Christians have is the thought that God is going to do what He wants no matter what they think. I choose not to believe that my Father, Best Friend and Savior doesn't care about how I feel about certain situations.

Think about your life and your friends and family members. When you are preparing to make a decision that will affect your family or friends, don't you get their input on the situation. Do you not care about how your decision will affect them or what they would like to do concerning your decision?

If you are a person who only looks out for yourself you are probably very lonely, and I would dare to say every relationship you have is completely circumstantial or superficial. Some adjectives that could describe these kinds of people would be selfish, self centered, conceited, lonely and, very likely, divorced.

51

Knowing this, let me ask you one question. Do these words accurately describe God our Father? I don't think so! Before we examine the above text let's look at another scripture as we try and identify God's character when dealing with our situations. Let's look at Matthew 7:8-11:

> *"For every one that asks receives; and he that seeks finds; and to him that knocks it shall be opened. Or what man is there of you, whom if his son ask bread, will he give him a stone? Or if he ask a fish, will he give him a serpent? If you then, being evil, know how to give good gifts unto your children, how much more shall your Father which is in heaven give good things to them that ask him?"*

Jesus makes His point about God's desire for our involvement with Him by asking how we deal with a child of ours making a request. Jesus asks (paraphrasing) "Is there any of you that would give your children a stone or serpent if they desire something to eat?" Jesus is trying to establish a foundation on which He can build a revelation of Himself. The foundation on which God builds revelation always begins with us allowing Him to get way down into the secret places of our hearts and reveal to us who we really are when no one else is around. This is called "integrity". This is the revelatory attribute Jesus reveals to us about His character through this scripture.

Integrity, in my opinion, is the basis of Christianity and even God Himself. Without it, you will never be trusted and with it you can never be stopped! If you don't believe and understand that everything God does, has done, says or has said is first sifted through the life found in Him alone, breathing through the lungs of integrity; you are living through a misconception that will suffocate the faith out of you.

Jesus first establishes the reaction of sinful men when making decisions concerning others. Then He says, "If you would make a decision to benefit someone else, how much more do you think a Holy God wants to make decisions according to your requests?"

What a powerful statement!

Basically, Jesus said, "I want you to have what you desire, according to My will for your life. All you have to do is give Me your input, because everyone that asks receives; and he that seeks finds; and to him that knocks it shall be opened."

Where in the Word of God does it say that God could care less about what I want out of my life? It doesn't, but that is what the world has taught us to think. If I have heard it once, I have heard it a dozen times. "God is going to do what He wants no matter what."

My only response to that is, ask the children of Israel why they stayed in the wilderness for so long when God had already given them Canaan. It was God's desire that His people inhabit the land He had created for them, but they chose to do it their own way. So it was their choices or input that kept them dwelling in a place that God intended for them to simply pass through.

I wonder how many times we end up living a lifestyle God never intended for us to live, but to just experience.

The truth is, God cares about how you feel concerning areas in your life.

After God created Adam, the Bible states that God brought the other living creatures to Adam. God then asked Adam what he wanted to name these creatures. This is how God deals with us even today. God has a plan and that plan has never changed; nor will it ever change. God's plan will come to pass. For instance, the "plan of salvation" was God's plan to reconcile His creation to Himself through His Son, Jesus. The plan happened and there is nothing – nor will there ever be anything – anyone can do to change it.

On the other hand, God also has a will concerning each of us. Unfortunately, His will has to change according to our input in situations. For a reference let's examine 2 Peter 3:9. It reads,

> *"The Lord is not slack concerning his promise, as some men count slackness; but is longsuffering to us-ward, not willing that any should perish, but that all should come to repentance."*

This shows us God's will is that no one should go to hell, but that everyone would repent and have an eternal relationship with Him. This is God's will, but this is not what happens in every case. God may will for us to prosper, but if we choose to sit home and complain or believe God is going to drop money in our mailbox, we will not prosper. God's will is for us to walk in health, but if we do not know His Word and respect His temple (our bodies), we will not achieve God's will.

So, then, God has to change his will according to our decisions. God's plan is eternal and never wavering. God's will is what is best for us, but according to our decisions it may or may not be accomplished in our lives.

The Lord is interested enough in your opinion to let you eat a stone even though He has prepared for you fresh bread. What we must decide is, do we want what God has willed for us or do we choose our destiny by what we feel is good for us?

I choose God's way instead of my own. I dare you to trust God even when everything inside you seems to pull you in the opposite direction. Your life will become *what you call it*!

Jeremiah 20:11 *"For I know the thoughts that I think toward you, saith the LORD, thoughts of peace, and not of evil, to give you an <u>expected end</u>."*

"As you are faithful, this one thing is certain, the Lord will show you great and mighty things that you know not now." (Stanley Frodsham)

I Am Beside Myself:

"And the LORD God caused a deep sleep to fall upon Adam, and he slept: and he took one of his ribs, and closed up the flesh instead thereof; And the rib, which the LORD God had taken from man, made he a woman, and brought her unto the man. And Adam said this is now bone of my bones, and flesh of my flesh: she shall be called Woman, because she was taken out of Man."
Genesis 2:21-23

————

Have you ever heard anyone say that someone is beside him or herself? This is what someone says about a person that is emotionally out of character, maybe because they are upset, excited or enthusiastic about a situation in their lives. This is what happened to Adam when God formed Eve from Adam's side.

The Bible said that God caused Adam to fall asleep and, from his side, God fashioned Eve. Adam then woke up to a sight never seen by man before or since; Adam saw himself sitting beside himself. His amazement was that Eve was flesh of his flesh and bone of his bone. She was him with a womb.

I would like to first reveal a nugget about God that we find evident in the creation of man and woman as two separate beings. Everything that exists was in God before He ever spoke the breath that created all things in Heaven and the Earth.

When I say everything was in God, I mean to say that God was, is and is to come (Revelation 1:4); therefore, if anything exists now, it had to be a part of God in the beginning. The Heavens, Earth and everything in them were alive in God in the beginning. God simply spoke and that which was a part of Him, by His breath, began to exist outside of Him. Notice I said everything exists outside of Him and not without Him.

Let's take this thought a little deeper as we examine a truth found in Proverbs 18:21: *"Death and life are in the power of the tongue..."*

In this scripture, part of God's image is identified to exist in men and women. God created everything with His words. Proverbs states that we have power to kill or bring life to situations in our lives by our words. That is a part of God's image we were created in. The power to speak life into things was created in mankind from the very beginning.

Remember, when God created the animals, He brought them to man and whatever Adam called them they became. What Adam was doing was flowing in his creative nature by speaking, bringing life and purpose to things around Him. Adam did not create the animals but he gave them meaning and life by explaining, if you will, what they were. It is very important for you to understand that something as simple as a word can change someone's life.

I can tell lots about the way parents speak to their children just by watching the child express himself or herself. For instance, children who have parents that constantly affirm them with positive words usually excel in most things they do. Their parents may affirm them with words such as *love, awesome, good, you can, great job*, or *I'm proud of you*. These words bring life and purpose to young people in search of who and what they are. They will grow up with positive belief in themselves, accomplishing almost everything set in front of them. All because the power of life was spoken into them through their parents.

On the other hand, you take children that constantly hear negative words spoken to them. Words like *stupid, nothing, worthless, dumb, ugly,* or *You are a brat,* just to name a few. These children have no self worth. They refuse to try because, what is the use of them trying when mom and dad have already identified them as stupid, worthless and good for nothing. They have no life or purpose in who they are.

This is a part of mankind that was not created in us from the beginning. Death does not exist anywhere in God's make up. Therefore, man was not created with the power in him to kill with his tongue.

So what happened, you may be asking?

Let me ask you a question in hope of prodding your memory. How did the devil trick Eve into partaking of the tree forbidden by God?

The serpent deceived with his words, right? The serpent took the words of life spoken to Adam by God and combined them with words that brought death to mankind. Thus, we now have not only the power to speak life and purpose to people and situations, but also the power to speak death to them. Adam, because of his creative nature, gave life and purpose to everything around him.

The reason I titled today's study, "I Am Beside Myself," is that we reproduce ourselves in the people and circumstances around us. We form them by the words we speak. If we are negative, grumpy and hateful people, the only people that will stay around us will be from the same mold. On the other hand, if we choose to speak words of love, life, comfort and adoration, those around us will be shaped by these words of life.

So wake up, look around and you will actually see yourself – beside yourself.

"If a child lives with criticism, he or she becomes a critic." (Author Unknown)

PART TWO

Why Me?
[The First Forming Process]

Destiny's Child:

"Before I formed thee in the belly I knew thee…"
Jeremiah 1:5

Isn't it wonderful to know that God knows who we are? This is a statement every Christian has heard but few really understand.

God cannot be viewed from the same eyes we use to see those around us. In our vernacular, to "know" someone is nothing more than making an acquaintance or remembering a name. If you were to ask your friend if he knows Mr. FlapJack, his response could be yes, even if he met him yesterday at the gas station. We apply a broad application concerning the idea of knowing a person.

However, even in our own vernacular, to know someone is to understand their thought process, or what they like to eat, what they do for fun, or maybe even knowing how many siblings they have. In reality, if we could answer these semi-intimate questions about others, from God's perspective we still wouldn't know the person. His "knowing" someone is far different from our own.

The word "knew" used in Jeremiah 1:5 comes from the Hebrew word "*yada*," which means to skillfully designate with an infinite understanding. It can actually mean to design or create your destiny. What God was saying to the prophet was that *BEFORE* He began to form him in his mother's womb, He created him with a destiny already established.

The fact is God did not create a destiny for any of us. On the contrary, He created us for a destiny.

That may sound very elementary, but to grasp this incredible truth about yourself, you must understand the order in which God chose to create you. **God's first decision was to create your destiny, then form you to fulfill that destiny**.

Look at Ephesians 1:11; it states,

"In whom also we have obtained an inheritance, being predestinated according to the purpose of him who worketh all things after the counsel of his own will."

In this scripture, we find that God has "predestinated" us according to His purpose. That word predestined is broken down like this. "Pre" means before or in the beginning, and "destine" means the end. So when it says that God predestined you, it means He first completed your ending before your life even began.

I am sure this may be hard for you to grasp. How can someone start at the end, when I don't even know what I will be doing in five minutes? Well, the only thing I can say is we are dealing with God, and He can do whatever He wills.

The great thing about all of this is the fact that you do have a purpose. That purpose does not exist in you, but rather it abides in who God is. This is why no matter how hard you try and fill the emptiness of your life, its thirst will never be quenched by anything other than God and

His purpose for you. You can fill your life with people, jobs, things, addictions or whatever. And you may become full, but you will never be fulfilled by them!

Praise God, for the fact that He has a destiny for you! You have a purpose for living each and every day of your life. No matter how many mistakes you make, no matter how many times you fall down, quit or miss the mark, God's destiny for you is still alive in you. That's because it wasn't formed in you. You, on the other hand, were given life through it.

I would like to take this moment and speak into your heart from the Lord.

I want to tell you to stand up on your feet and go after that which you desire for your life. You may have been told, or maybe you feel like, you were a "mistake" or that your parents didn't plan to have you. Let me start by saying that doesn't make a hill of beans! (That, by the way, is good old *country slang* for "It doesn't matter.") If you are here on this Earth, reading this book, God says you are not a mistake.

On the contrary, you have a purpose and a destiny that can only be found in God. God and all the host of Heaven and everything in it, are cheering you on to victory. There are no circumstances, people or devils that can stop you from accomplishing your destiny when God is for you.

Remember Romans 8:31: "*If God be for us, who can be against us?*"

You are not a mistake, but rather a masterpiece. **There are no walls to keep you from your destiny, but rather the walls are to make you climb higher**. God knows you. He created you, and even more, He created a destiny that you can only accomplish through Him!

That's right; your destiny can only be accomplished through God.

"You mean, God has created me with purpose, for a destiny, but that doesn't mean I will automatically accomplish it?"

You are correct. People think that since God has predestined us, we will just somehow, even accidentally, achieve our destiny. Remember in one of the previous chapters I informed you that God allows Himself to be limited by two things: His Word and man's will. The truth is, God can do whatever He wants, but He limits Himself to do what the Bible says and what man wills for his life.

I could have ended this chapter by pumping you up with the truth about God having created you with a destiny, but that wouldn't do a whole lot of good if you think you can live any way you want and blame God for your failures.

The fact is God has a destiny for you, and He leads you to that destiny by placing desires in your heart and people in your life, and He brings everything together by times and seasons. **If you choose to live by wrong desires and around the wrong people, you will be choosing a different destiny outside of God's perfect will for your life**.

In Romans chapter 12, we learn that God has a good, an acceptable and a perfect will for our lives. We must strive to achieve the perfect will of God. This desire will not allow you to accept the good or the acceptable will of God, and will lead you into achieving the destiny you were created for. The easy way isn't always the best way.

God is a God that wants to be chosen as He has chosen us. He is looking for a people, who will be faithful to Him, as He is always faithful to us. If you believe God has a destiny for you, the understanding and the desire to achieve His perfect destiny for your life will strengthen you to always be faithful to God. Faithfulness isn't fulfilled over a weekend. That is called a "fling." On the other hand, faithfulness is birthed only through the decision to stick by someone through thick and thin, good and bad, hell and high water. That is faithfulness, and that is the way a "Child of Destiny" chooses to live.

"Change your thoughts and you change your world."
(Norman Vincent Peale)

"What's Going on in There?"

"…and before you came forth out of the womb I sanctified thee…" Jeremiah 1:5

———

Have you ever thought about what is happening in a mother when she is pregnant? I know we understand through science that the baby is growing eyes, arms, legs and hair, but where does its gender come from? Or better yet what determines the baby's eye color, hair color or size?

Again we can read books that will tell us that the gender of the child is determined by the dominant sperm cells or the hair color is determined by the child's grandmother. Listen, I am not trying to downplay the wisdom of men and women of today through my ignorance of human and medical science. On the contrary, what I would like to show you through the Word of God is that God uses all the cells, genetic makeup and whatever else it takes for humans to exist, to create us. Who we are and the makeup of our physical bodies are created by the breath of God, through the infinite wisdom of God, directed toward preparing us for our destiny.

We read in yesterday's section that before we were in our mother's womb, God created a destiny, then He created us for that destiny.

Today we see that God takes the process of our creation a step further. God now goes from dealing with the forming process *before* we were in the womb to the forming that happens while we are *in* our mother's womb.

God told Jeremiah, *"Before you were created in the womb I knew you, and before you came out of the womb I sanctified you."*

Again, God wasn't just blabbing some hocus pocus to Jeremiah in this text. He was instilling purpose within Jeremiah by unveiling the process of creation to him. He told Jeremiah, while you were in the womb, I "sanctified" you. Let's take a moment for the sake of conversation and explore the meaning of the word "sanctify," as used here in Jeremiah chapter 1.

The Hebrew word for sanctify used in this scripture is the word *"qadash,"* which translates to "prepare." The Lord was saying to Jeremiah, "Before I formed you in the womb I created for you a destiny, and while you were in the womb I prepared you with all the talents, abilities and everything you need to accomplish that destiny." This sounds like a God of preparation, doesn't it?

What a liberating truth, to know that God created me with a destiny already set, and then, while in the womb He formed me with everything I need to accomplish that destiny!

Isn't God so good?

Think about the fact that God formed you in your mother's womb as somebody before you ever took your first breath. You are somebody not because of what you do, but solely because of what He did. Remember this the next time you feel inadequate, good for nothing or lacking. You are not lacking in any way, shape or form!

70

God created you – or better yet, He "SANCTIFIED" you – before the doctor ever slapped you on the bottom.

When you look at yourself in a displeasing fashion and say things such as, "I am ugly," or "I am not smart or talented enough," you are telling God that He didn't do a good enough job. How would you like to stand in the presence of the almighty God and say, "Thanks for nothing!"?

That would not be a very intelligent statement, would it? But that is what you do every time you look down on, or degrade yourself.

God has fashioned you to look like you do, have the talents you have, live in the region where you live and live in this time period for His purpose. There are no accidents with God. Nothing just happens; neither does anything catch God by surprise. You are you because God formed you to be you. (That was a mouthful!)

God had great things in store for Jeremiah. God's will for Jeremiah, however, would not have done much good if Jeremiah didn't know He had great things for him to do with his life.

See, it's one thing for God or someone else to see greatness in you, but it does little good if you don't see that greatness for yourself.

Before we end our discussion today, let me share one more scripture with you.

In Luke 10:27, we read a quote from Jesus concerning the greatest commandment from God. It states,

"You shall love the Lord your God with all your heart, and with all your soul, and with all your strength, and with all your mind; and your neighbor as yourself."

This scripture is very plain in its commandment for us to love God and *our neighbors as we love ourselves.*

71

My question for you is, how can you love God and your neighbor if you don't love yourself?

The answer is, according to this verse, "You can't!"

If you can't look in the mirror every morning and say, "I love you," to yourself, then it is impossible to truly love anyone or anything else. Love yourself for who you are.

God does.

My prayer is that the next time you see a pregnant woman, your true identity will erupt within you because of the truth within this chapter about God's forming process of equipping you for success. Success is not a destination, but a journey. You came into this world a success and you shall leave this world a success. God knows it, and I know it.

The only question that remains is, do you know it?

"The biggest disease today is not leprosy or tuberculosis, but rather the feeling of being unwanted, uncared for and deserted by everybody." (Mother Theresa)

"Push!"

———

If you were to ask any woman in labor what one word is on her mind at the point of birth, that word would be "PUSH." My wife and I have been through two pregnancies, and I've learned that when it's time to give birth, the most natural urge the woman senses is the urge to push. The woman does not have to remember to push, nor does she need someone to teach her to push, it just comes naturally.

This is the last step God showed Jeremiah about the process of forming us in the womb. The word, "ordained," found here in our text is the Hebrew word, *"nathan,"* which means, "to cause to bring forth or to push."

My prayer is that the last two days, as well as today, will change your life as it did the Prophet Jeremiah's life. Jeremiah was never the same after God revealed to him the forming process in which God created him with a destiny and equipped him for that destiny. When he was prepared, God literally pushed him out to his destiny.

73

To think God took that much time in forming you! He ordained your ending, prepared you never to fail, but to always succeed. Then to top it all off, God would not allow you to be born until this process was perfectly completed. Then and only then did God push or catapult you forth into your destiny.

I also found during my adventures in labor that it takes two people in a labor and delivery room. It takes one person to push and one to pull. God has shown His hand, identifying His job as pushing. Therefore, our job must be to pull. You may be asking yourself what I mean by saying your job is to pull. You may be asking, "How can I pull on myself when I already exist?"

Let me make myself clear. God created you for a destiny, then he equipped you with everything you need to accomplish that destiny. Finally, God took you and pushed you forward in the direction of your destiny. Your job now is to pull on the wisdom of God for guidance to direct you to your destiny.

The Bible says in James 1:5, "*If any of you lack wisdom, let him ask of God, that gives to all men liberally, and upbraids not; and it shall be given him.*" What is the wisdom James is talking about?

Well I am glad you asked. Let's take this journey a little further.

In James, chapter 1, the writer begins his letter dealing with the times when we face trials and tribulations in this world. James says things like, "*count it all joy when you fall into different temptations,*" and "the *trying of your faith is more precious than that of gold.*" When I read this, my fleshly mind wants to say, "Whatever! I can't be happy when I am in a trial."

You probably can relate to what I am saying and if not, you have been blessed with more faith than I have ever seen.

But what James is saying is, if you understand why we go through trials and tribulations it will bring joy to your life. Let me explain.

Trials are not allowed in our lives to hurt or kill us, but to direct us toward our destiny. I heard one man say it like this, "If you are facing an enemy, you are facing God's promotion program."

Take King David, for instance. He was just a little shepherd boy when he was chosen by God and anointed to be the king of Israel. But it was years later when he actually became king.

As a matter of fact, the event that "pushed" David into his destined throne was the victory over an enemy named Goliath. Some people would have cried and said, "Woe is me; God is mad at me because I am facing this great trial."

Not David; he knew that God had promised him the throne and nothing was going to stand in the way of him reaching his destiny.

David didn't have any military training, and he had no family support, but he had faith in his ability through God. For you to pull down the wisdom and destiny of God, you have got to believe in your abilities through faith in God.

David told King Saul when asked how he was going to defeat this enemy, *"Thy servant kept his father's sheep, and there came a lion, and a bear, and took a lamb out of the flock. And I went out after him, and smote him, and delivered it out of his mouth. Then he arose against me, I caught him by his beard, and smote him, and slew him. Thy servant slew both the lion and the bear: and this uncircumcised Philistine shall be as one of them, seeing he hath defied the armies of the living God."*

I believe that something clicked inside David and he realized that God had been preparing him through trials and tribulations. Preparing him for what, you may ask. God was preparing David for his throne.

Great people are fashioned by great enemies. The bigger the giant the larger the promotion. Only people who know who they are in the eyes of God can live life with this kind of mindset. God has pushed you toward your destiny, but you have got to pull yourself to it. Wimps never reach their destiny. It takes strong men and women with a fight on the inside of them to pull even when it hurts.

You may be facing one of these times of trial and you have been "pulling," but your arms are numbed from the struggle. I speak to you by the Spirit when I say, "Hold On!" Even if you can't pull, just don't let go of the rope. A wise man once said, "When you get to the end of your rope, tie a knot in the bottom of it."

The Bible states it even more clearly in Ephesians 6:13 when it says, *"Wherefore take unto you the whole armor of God, that you may be able to withstand in the evil day, and having done all, to stand."*

Hold on, keep fighting, or stand! Just don't let go, give up or sit down. Your destiny is too important to let what is meant to exalt you kill you. This is not meant for your destruction but for your promotion!

Always remember Galatians 6:9: *"And let us not be weary in well doing: for in due season we shall reap, if we faint not."*

"The nose of a bulldog is slanted backwards so it can continue to breathe without letting go." (Winston Churchill)

No More "I Can't":

"Then said I, Ah, Lord GOD! Behold, I cannot speak: for I am a child. But the LORD said unto me, Say not, I am a child: for you shall go to all that I shall send thee, and whatsoever I command thee you shall speak." Jeremiah 1:6 & 7

"Can't is the brother of *I don't want to."* This is a favorite cliché of one of my former associate pastors. Though this statement may sound a little bold or even harsh, the underlying fact behind this combination of negative words is powerfully true. If you would take a moment to dwell on this statement, I believe a liberty would come to your life that you may have been desiring for a long time.

You may be asking yourself, "How will liberty come from my simply thinking on this one-liner?"

Let me explain by using two one-liners found in the Word of God.

The first scripture is John 4:24. It says,

"God is a Spirit: and they that worship him must worship him in spirit and in truth."

The second is found in 2 Corinthians 3:17, which states,

"Now the Lord is that Spirit: and where the Spirit of the Lord is, there is liberty."

The Bible explains two things as we combine these scriptures. First, if we are going to get into the presence of the Lord, where change, fulfillment and self worth come, we must be truthful to our self and with God.

Second, when we become honest and truthful with ourselves, then and only then is the Spirit of God attracted to us. And where the Spirit of the Lord is, that life becomes liberated.

The process of being set free, delivered, or whatever you want to call it when the Spirit of the Lord liberates a person, always begins with the truth. When people begin a sentence with the words, "I can't," what they are saying is, I don't want to deal with the truth. Truth is at the essence of everything God is and stands for.

In the book of Revelation, chapter nineteen, it states that God is "Faithful and True." God exists in truth. That is why, when God says something, it happens. There is absolute truth and faith in His words. They cannot fail to form what He speaks. Therefore, if I want God to do something in my heart and life, I must be honest with Him and myself.

Actually, the word "can't" is not in God's vocabulary. When you say, "I can't," to God, as Jeremiah did, there is only one thing that happens. That is, you become bound to the pain of your situation even more than before. It is not God's fault, idea or His will for this to happen. You bring this on yourself when you hide the truth along with the pain, insecurity and fear of rejection that is being suppressed by not dealing with the truth.

It seems a lot easier and more painless to say you can't than to deal with what you could do if you would "let go and let God."

I want to take this a step further if you *can* stand to hear the *truth*.

In Ephesians chapter 6, while describing the spiritual armor Christians are to adorn themselves with, the Apostle Paul describes part of our armor as having our *"loins girt about with truth..."* The "loins" are reproductive organs, meaning the sole function of the loins is to provide whatever is needed to reproduce. Knowing this, we find that part of our armor is to protect the reproductive organ of our spirit.

Isn't it funny that the armor that protects our reproductive organ is the armor of "truth"? What the writer is telling us is to be honest with ourselves because honesty will reproduce honesty, just like a lie will reproduce a lie.

Let me ask you a question that may help us catch this rabbit. Have you ever told a lie? Your answer will probably be yes. My next question is, then, did you have to tell another lie to cover up that lie? Yes, again, I suppose. Do you know why your situation could not be handled with one lie? Because truth reproduces truth and lies reproduce lies. It is the law of nature. Once you begin to lie, it gets easier and more frequent, and eventually it becomes a lifestyle, so much so that you will even begin to believe the lie yourself.

Have you ever heard the term, "living a lie"? This is when someone is living so far from the truth that they even begin to think they are living out their purpose in life. Thus, they create someone that God doesn't even know.

Oh, I know what you are thinking. "Nothing was created that God didn't create and know."

Maybe I can prove my point by once again going to the Word of God. The scripture does say in Ephesians 3:9 that God created all things by Jesus Christ. I would love to go into detail on the meaning of this scripture, but my assignment today limits me to briefly making the statement that God did create everything before the fall of man. After sin entered into the world, sin itself begin to "create," if you will, things God had nothing to do with.

For example, God didn't make Satan. (Oh yeah, it is about to get good. I can sense liberation beginning to leap from the words on this page even as I am writing them.) God created an angel whose name was Lucifer. So where did Satan come from?

I am glad you asked. Lucifer began to believe a lie that produced or created Satan. In Isaiah 14:13-14, the prophet is speaking of Lucifer when saying, *"For you have said in your heart, 'I will ascend into heaven, I will exalt my throne above the stars of God. I will sit also upon the mount of the congregation, in the sides of the north. I will ascend above the heights of the clouds and I will be like the most High.'"*

God didn't create Satan. Lucifer created Satan when he began to believe his own lie.

Have you ever wondered why an all knowing, infinite, everlasting, eternal, self-existing God would ask a man He created, "Where are you?" The reason is that when Adam and Eve ate the fruit of a lie, they became that lie. In other words, the lie the serpent told Adam and Eve produced a race that God didn't create. They were not what they were created to be, but they became sinners because of a lie. This is why the Spirit of an all knowing, infinite, everlasting, eternal, self-existing God did not recognize beings He had created with His own breath. The image that God created them in was now changed into the likeness of sin, re-created by dishonesty.

God had just gotten through showing Jeremiah who we were created to be and his first word after this awesome revelation was, "*I can't, because I do not know how to speak. I am only a child.*"

I wonder if you are living a lie and not living up to who God has created you to be. Maybe your life is so disguised by what the lie of "I can't" has produced that you don't even know who God created you to be. Maybe you want to be true with yourself, but the truth is something that is hidden somewhere between what you desire in your heart and what you see with your eyes.

What is the truth? What has God created you and me to be? Let me tell you the truth. It is found in Deuteronomy 28:1-13.

> "*If you fully obey the LORD your God and carefully follow all his commands I give you today, the LORD your God will set you high above all the nations on earth. All these blessings will come upon you and accompany you if you obey the LORD your God: You will be blessed in the city and blessed in the country. The fruit of your womb will be blessed, and the crops of your land and the young of your livestock – the calves of your herds and the lambs of your flocks. Your basket and your kneading trough will be blessed. You will be blessed when you come in and blessed when you go out. The LORD will grant that the enemies who rise up against you will be defeated before you. They will come at you from one direction but flee from you in seven. The LORD will send a blessing on your barns and on everything you put your hand to. The LORD your God will bless you in the land he is giving you. The LORD will establish you as his holy people, as he promised you on oath, if you keep the commands of the LORD your God and walk in his ways. Then all the peoples on earth will*

see that you are called by the name of the LORD, and they will fear you. The LORD will grant you abundant prosperity – in the fruit of your womb, the young of your livestock and the crops of your ground – in the land he swore to your forefathers to give you. The LORD will open the heavens, the storehouse of his bounty, to send rain on your land in season and to bless all the work of your hands. You will lend to many nations but will borrow from none. The LORD will make you the head, not the tail. If you pay attention to the commands of the LORD your God that I give you this day and carefully follow them, you will always be at the top, never at the bottom."

This is who God created you to be! Therefore, there is no more, "I can't."

"Always tell the truth, and you will never have to remember what you said." (T.L. Osborn)

He Wouldn't Ask You if He Wouldn't Prepare You:

"But the LORD said to me, 'Do not say, "I am only a child." You must go to everyone I send you to and say whatever I command you.'" Jeremiah 1:7

———

I believe one of the most frightening feelings a person could ever experience is to feel inadequate. When you feel inadequate or unprepared an almost paralyzing sensation will attack your mind. You will lose your ability to think clearly. Your decision making is impaired and who you are begins to bow to the pressure of not measuring up to the standards surrounding you at that time.

Through my time of ministry I have come in contact with many different people – people of different color, nationality, background and income level, but one thing is the same in everyone. We all are afraid of failure and rejection. The thought of failing and being rejected has a grip on people that is stronger than any thing outside of the Spirit and the power of God.

When I began to think about this stronghold, the shepherd in me couldn't help but ask why, and what I can do to help. To find my answer, as usual, I reverted to the Word of God. So let's take a moment and search the scripture in hope of finding our answer when confronted with the feeling of inadequacy.

In 2 Chronicles 30:36, the Bibles says,

"And Hezekiah rejoiced, and all the people, that God had prepared the people: for the thing was done suddenly."

Throughout the majority of the Word of God, we can read how God is a God of preparation. Nothing catches Him by surprise. Here, in the above text, King Hezekiah and the people of God were facing an enemy that came upon them quickly and suddenly. There wasn't much time for preparation or planning. They didn't even have time to protect themselves. The only thing they could do was put their crisis in the Lord's hand.

I am sure when the men and women of God saw their enemy bearing down on them suddenly, without any warning, they felt inadequate and even rejected by God. I am sure the thought of failure was dominating their minds. The easiest thing for them to do, I'm sure, would have been to wave the white flag, give up and blame God for their destruction.

However, they chose to believe God and do what He said. Victory came that day to the men and women of God not because they believed in themselves, but they chose to believe that if God was for them, who could be against them! (Romans 8:31)

The Bible states that the king and the people were filled with joy. Now, we can relate to this feeling of joy that the people experienced because they had just obtained victory through a battle. But the scripture doesn't say they were filled with joy because of their victory. The Bible makes it very clear why the people were filled with joy. They were filled with joy because "*God had prepared the people.*"

These were the same people who, shortly before, were in a panic because their enemy sneaked up on them and they felt inadequate, unprepared and vulnerable. They didn't know what God knew. What God knew was that He had already prepared them for any and everything that they would ever face in this world. Joy filled their hearts because they overcame an obstacle that they were scared of and *felt* unprepared to fight.

You may be reading this while facing a trial or enemy that you *feel* unprepared to overcome. You may be feeling lonely, frustrated or inadequate.

I tell you in the name of Jesus, you are not alone, nor have you been set up to fail. God will never ask you to do anything that He hasn't already completely and thoroughly equipped you for. Remember, every enemy is a road sign to a greater glory in God.

Lastly, I would like to explain to you one other reason mankind "shuts down" at the sense of inadequacy.

Our feelings of being adequate have such a negative effect because inadequacy goes against our created nature, the part of our inner being that remembers God. What I mean is, Adam was created with the natural ability to have dominion and victory in every situation. The feeling of being inadequate or experiencing fear of rejection comes from sin. The Bibles says the wages of sin is death, and death is assured to people who don't believe in the God who cleanses us of sin. You have nothing to fear. God is your Father, Jesus is your Savior, and the Holy Spirit is your Guide. With that being said, you can go where God tells you to go, and say what He tells you to say, because He will never ask you to do anything that you are not prepared to accomplish.

Philippians 4:13 says *"I can do all things through Christ which strengtheneth me."*

"All great discoveries have been made by people whose faith ran ahead of their minds." (John L. Mason)

You Were Not Created to Fear Anything:

"Do not be afraid of them, for I am with you and will rescue you, declares the LORD." Jeremiah 1:8

———

What are you afraid of?

This is a very broad question, but I would like to go on record stating my belief that fear is the primary factor behind most of our failures in life. We are afraid of rejection, people's opinions, losing, winning, not being strong enough, being too strong – we are even afraid of failure itself. Fear has a grip that is tighter than the strongest cord ever made. It seems to have an astounding perseverance, and fear also seems to know your times of weakness.

Fear is like an unwanted friend who shows up at the party and takes control. It begins to organize the functions, make all the decisions and has a voice louder than any other in the room. Everyone in the room with fear unknowingly enters into a hypnotic state under its control.

You are probably nodding your head right now in agreement with me.

If you're not, it is simply because you have not identified your problem as fear. You probably think your life is falling apart because it's God's will, your spouse's fault or maybe it is just in your genetic make-up. These are all good hiding places for fear.

See, fear will control you and not even use its real identity. Fear is like the devil; he doesn't care who or what you serve as long as you don't serve God. And fear doesn't care what you classify it as, just as long as its effect is destruction.

Have you ever wondered why fear seems to grip you every time you have a big decision to make in your life? Do you know why? Fear is the flesh's or the devil's way of silencing the voice and direction of God in your life.

We have read in the previous chapters how God created us for a destiny and how He created us with everything we will ever need to achieve that destiny. One of the things God created us for was to be victorious in every area of our lives, and the main thing we are to accomplish these victories with is the ability to KNOW His voice and direction.

One of the hardest things for people to do today is make decisions. Though we are faced with decision every day, most people do not have the ability to make good Biblical decisions. Why? Is it because God did not give us the ability to make good decisions? No, it's because fear declares war against your creative ability as a human to make a distinctive, unhindered decision when confronted with any problem.

As we discussed earlier, after Adam was created, the first thing he began to do was make decisions. Adam had to decide how to take care of the Garden of Eden. He had to name all the animals.

As a matter of fact, it was his decision to eat of the forbidden fruit that brought sin and separated him from his Creator. Your Bible says that Eve was deceived, but Adam was presented with a choice. God told him that the consequence of eating of the forbidden tree was death. This was the decision Adam faced after his wife ate of the tree herself. Adam didn't have to eat of the fruit. He could have said, "No, you go ahead and die on your own." But he didn't.

I believe Adam's desire to please God was tainted by the fear of being alone again, or of not pleasing his wife or maybe even by the fear of not being loyal to God's gift to him. Whatever it was, you can bet the voice of fear could be heard throughout Paradise on that dreadful day.

God created mankind with the natural ability to make good decisions. Fear, however, will bring doubt to you when you are confronted with a decision, not just so you don't make the correct decision, but more so to silence the voice of God from your *ears*.

Adam never struggled with hearing the voice of the Lord until he made one wrong decision. That decision caused a chain reaction birth into sin that combats every decision we make even until today. The fear of being incorrect, wrongfully judged or hurt has a seemingly silent yet deadly cry, commissioned by sin to keep you from your destiny.

The good news is that there is a voice that cries for you that is louder than the cry of fear. That cry is the cry of love.

The love of God shouts louder than any sound, voice or cry that will ever present itself to you. The love of God shouts your innocence even when you make a bad decision. It seems to scream forgiveness, truth, acceptance and honor even when you have the sensation of being worthless, filthy and cast out.

We are a people with limitations. Time, space, feelings and abilities limit us. What I mean is, everything we do, say and feel is limited by what we know. Therefore, we only have the ability to love to a certain degree and then our love fails.

Take Peter for instance. His love for Jesus was proven time and time again. He walked on the angry waves of a storm-tossed sea because he wanted to be with Jesus. It was Peter who risked a death penalty by cutting off a Roman soldier's ear all because the man grabbed Jesus' arm. Wasn't it Peter who tried to hold back days of fatigue all because Jesus asked him to pray with Him in the Garden of Gethsemane?

Peter loved Jesus as much as anyone, and more than most. But it was this same Peter who denied knowing Jesus while standing at the gate of the temple after Jesus was arrested and put on trial. Again he denied his relationship with the Lord, standing by a fire when recognized by a few cool civilians. The failing of his love was complete when he denied even knowing Jesus as he was confronted by a teenage girl.

Peter's love started him on his journey toward a successful life and relationship with Christ, but because of fear and the limitations of being human, it failed him.

Thank God that the story doesn't end with the love that only starts. It ends with a love that finishes.

Even after Peter denied knowing Jesus three times; even after he returned to doing what God had called him out of – that is, fishing – he encountered a greater love than his own. Jesus met Peter on the rocky banks of his favorite fishing hole one evening. He didn't condemn him, judge him or even bring up his past. Jesus simply offered Peter something even fear had no strength against: the kind of love that finishes!

You may be reading this book under the pressure of deadlines, expectations or worries, but I speak peace to you, knowing that if you make the right decision or the wrong decision, the love of God will finish in you what He has begun. This is the only effective weapon against fear.

I John 4:18 says, *"Perfect love casts out all fear."*

That is the weapon of knowing God's love, knowing it will lead you, forgive you and start you over again if need be. Whatever it takes, the love that finishes will fight for you, if you will call on it.

This was God's heart toward Jeremiah when He told him not to fear, "...for I am with you." Fear has no effect on a person who has experienced the love of God and who knows that it is this love that created him in the first place. God has created you by His love and He will finish or perfect you with the same.

Fear not, you shall succeed!

Psalms 27:1-5 says,

"The LORD is my light and my salvation – whom shall I fear? The LORD is the stronghold of my life – of whom shall I be afraid? When evil men advance against me to devour my flesh, when my enemies and my foes attack me, they will stumble and fall. Though an army besiege me, my heart will not fear; though war break out against me, even then will I be confident. One thing I ask of the LORD, this is what I seek: that I may dwell in the house of the LORD all the days of my life, to gaze upon the beauty of the LORD and to seek him in his temple. For in the day of trouble he will keep me safe in his dwelling; he will hide me in the shelter of his tabernacle and set me high upon a rock."

"The difference in someone experiencing success and a fulfilled life, and one of a less fortunate pathway, is all

determined by their ability to silence the voice of fear."
(David Edmondson)

Choosing to Remember What God Has *Already* Done:

"Then the LORD put forth his hand, and touched my mouth. And the LORD said unto me, Behold, I have put my words in thy mouth." Jeremiah 1:9

———

One of the hardest things in life is to do as Paul taught us in Philippians 3:13-14.

That scripture says:

"Brethren, I count not myself to have apprehended: but this one thing I do, forgetting those things which are behind, and reaching forth unto those things which are before. I press toward the mark for the prize of the high calling of God in Christ Jesus."

I know what you are thinking. It is a lot easier to *say* you are forgetting past failures and hurts than to *actually* forget them.

Have you ever wondered why God doesn't wipe away the memory of your past when He wipes away and forgets your sins? I mean, if God is so good and He is big enough to cleanse me of my sins, why doesn't He sweep clean the dirty images of my past?

The reason is, God doesn't want you to forget where He has brought you.

Romans 2:4 says it is the goodness of God that "leads thee to repentance." God's goodness is revealed at its greatest when He takes your life of failure, condemnation and death, then gives you a new life to start over.

That is what Paul taught us in 2 Corinthians 5:17 when he said, *"Therefore if any man be in Christ, he is a new creature. Old things are passed away. Behold, all things are become new."*

What he is saying is when you ask Jesus into your heart, your spirit becomes clean and even brand new through the blood of Jesus. That is why Paul could say after you ask Jesus into your life, you become a "new creature."

We know that our fleshly body doesn't change, nor do a lot of our situations. The things that do change are that you receive eternal life, your sins are forgiven and forgotten and your spiritual position takes up residence in God, as well as many more things that I could list.

But I think you see what I am getting at. The thing that instantly changes is the condition of who you really are, which is your spirit man.

Let us take this thought a little deeper for just a moment.

Let me begin by asking you: How does God receive glory from your life?

I know what you may be thinking. "God gets glory out of our lives in many ways." I understand that concept, but there is one way that God receives glory from your life, and it stands head and shoulders above the rest. The way I think God gets the most glory from your life is when He takes your life that you have made a mess of and makes something out of nothing. The greatest testimony for God is when someone has made a series of bad decisions, his life is falling apart and he has no hope, but Jesus takes that mess and makes the person a success. This is one reason God doesn't allow the memory of the past to be obliterated. God is glorified when you – and the people you know – remember you as you were, while seeing who you have become.

There is yet another reason God will not let you forget your past: so you will have hope to press on toward all His goals for you, toward the mark for the prize of the high calling in Christ. Your imperfections, the knowledge that your flesh has the potential to choose to go back to that life, and heart-felt thankfulness at His deliverance – these draw you to more grace at the mercy seat of God. You know that if it had not been for God and His mercy, you would still be a lost, broken and empty person in need of a Savior.

Thank God you can remember what it was like to be lonely, broken, strung out, sinful and Fatherless!

As long as you don't forget where you have been, you will never lose track of where you are going. Don't focus on your past, but you definitely need to remember it.

The way we "press toward the mark for the prize of the high calling in Christ" is not to dwell on what God hasn't yet done in our lives. On the contrary, we must think of what he has already done for us.

If you will remind yourself of what God has done for you, belief for what God is going to do will come easy. God told Jeremiah "I have put my words in your mouth." God didn't tell him what he was going to do for him. God knew if He could get the prophet to understand what He had already done, the rest would fall into place. This truth can be uncovered even better as we look into the Word of God.

In the book of Mark, chapter 6, the disciples were traveling to Bethsaida when they encountered a very bad storm. The ship they were in was being tossed about and even began to sink. Jesus was on land when He looked out and saw what was going on. When He noticed that His disciples were in trouble, He left the comfort of land and began to walk on the water to save His friends.

Let me go back for just a moment to the events leading up to this encounter, so that we can be on the same page. Remember that, only a few hours before, Jesus performed a mighty miracle by feeding thousands of people with some fish and bread. Then He sent His disciples into the boat to cross over the Sea of Galilee.

When the disciples found themselves alone in a storm, they looked out across the raging sea just in time to see Jesus walking on the water toward them. Unfortunately, they didn't know it was Jesus. The Bible says they actually thought it was a spirit, which raised another issue all together. Jewish tradition said that if you were in a storm while out on the sea and you saw a spirit, your ship was going to sink and everyone on board would die.

What do you think you would have done if you were in their situation? Probably the same thing I would have done, which is what they did. They began to cry out, "We're going to die and God doesn't even care."

Maybe they didn't say those exact words, but that is probably what you and I would have said.

When I read this scripture, I can't help but ask myself why they didn't know this was Jesus walking toward them. They knew Him better than anybody else did. They ate, traveled and lived with Jesus. They should have known it was Jesus, don't you think? Well, the answer to our question is found in Mark 6:52. It says they did not recognize Jesus because *they considered not the miracle of the loaves: for their heart was hardened.*

They got their eyes on their circumstances and forgot the miracle working power of Jesus, which He had just revealed to them a couple of hours earlier. They forgot what God had already done.

It is very dangerous to live by what you see instead of remembering where you have been.

You may be in the middle of a storm, tossed back and forth, with black skies all around, with no apparent end in sight. You may not know how you are going to make it to the other side.

This one thing is true: God does know, and He has promised you that He will make a way for you where there seems to be no way.

Refuse to look at where you are or what you need for God to do.

Remember what He has already done in your life and know that He is the same yesterday, today and forever. If He has brought you this far, He will finish taking you all the way to the other side.

Victory is at your water's edge. The same water that is raging today will become calm and be refreshment for you tomorrow.

Oh yes, before we are finished for today, guess what happened when the disciples and Jesus got to the other side?

They brought freedom to a man who had been tormented, cast out and alone for years.

Remember, the enemy never fights someone he is not scared of.

One of my favorite scriptures is found in Philippians 1:6: *"Being confident of this very thing, that he which hath begun a good work in you will perform it until the day of Jesus Christ."*

"Don't accept your present, temporary situations as your future, permanent situations." (John Mason)

PART THREE

Servant Jacob and Chosen Israel
(The Second Forming Process)

You Get What You Accept:

"And Jacob was left alone; and there wrestled a man with him until the breaking of the day." Genesis 32:24

———

As we begin the final and most liberating part of God's process of forming us to be what He created us to be, we must examine the background of a man named Jacob.

Jacob was the son of Isaac and Rebecca. He had a brother named Esau, who was older than Jacob. Because Esau was the elder brother of Jacob, he had the right to receive the blessing of his father when his father died. The blessing of the father consisted of many things which I do not have time to go into, but it can be summed up for the sake of conversation by saying, Esau would have most of the family royalty and most of the power.

Isaac was on his deathbed ready to pass down the family blessing to his eldest son Esau, when Rebecca, who wanted Jacob to receive the blessing, devised a plan to trick Isaac into blessing Jacob instead of Esau. (I would like to point out to you that it was not Jacob's idea, but it was his mother's idea.) So Rebecca devised a scam to trick Isaac into blessing Jacob.

She had Jacob dress up in a furry coat and go into his father's room to feed him. She had him dress in a fur coat because Esau was a very hairy man, and when Isaac touched Jacob he would feel the hair and think it was Esau. To make a long story short, Jacob went along with the scam even though he did not want to. That was just the way he was. Whatever came his way, he just bowed his head to the pressure and took the easy way out.

After stealing Esau's birthright, Rebecca came to Jacob again and instructed him to flee for his life. She told him to go and live with her brother, Laban, and his family. Again, I'm sure Jacob did not want to leave all of his friends and family, but as before, he just tucked his tail and went on his way.

Upon arriving at his new home, Jacob met a woman who was named Rachel and he fell in love with her at the first glimpse. So he went to Laban and asked for her hand in marriage. Laban and Jacob agreed that after Jacob worked for Laban seven years, he could have Rachel as his wife.

Now, you must understand that Rachel was fine. The Bible says she was beautiful. So Jacob agreed to the seven-year deal for Rachel, whom he loved.

Imagine working seven years for a paycheck. Every day while working, you think of that check and how good it is going to feel when you get it in your hands and cash it. You would probably wake up every morning and go to bed every night thinking of your money. While talking with friends, the paycheck you are working so hard for would always get brought up in every conversation. This must have been the way Jacob spent his days and nights for seven years, his mind filled with Rachel's face. Every day he would wake up early to go and see her do her chores and watch her converse with her friends. I mean, he had to love and desire to be with this woman to wait seven long years for her.

Do you know that seven years works out to be 84 months, or 364 weeks, or 2555 days, or 61,320 hours? That is a long time to wait for anything, don't you think? But Jacob waited. For seven years he worked for Laban to receive his daughter's hand in marriage.

After those seven years, can guess what happened? Laban tricked Jacob by giving him his other daughter, Leah, instead of Rachel as they agreed.

Let me stop here for just a minute and give you some advice as I am reminded of an old cliché. "What goes around comes around."

Don't feel sorry for Jacob, because he simply reaped from the same seeds he sowed. The point I want to make here is that Jacob had no backbone. He just accepted everything that life brought his way. When Jacob realized that he had been given the wrong woman he accepted it and agreed to work another seven years for Rachel.

I could go on and on about Jacob and his lack of self-confidence and character, but I think you are getting the point. I will, however, tell you that while Jacob was working for Laban, God blessed Jacob so much that Laban ended up changing his wage ten times. Guess what? Jacob accepted it every time without the least fight.

Also, when Rachel was barren and could not have any children, Jacob had children with the handmaidens of his wives, even when he didn't want to, all because Rachel asked him to. And you know Jacob; he said, sure whatever you want me to do. This was Jacob, a soft, weak, lowly, pride-less young man who had no fight in him for what he desired in life.

Maybe you can relate to this man named Jacob. I mean, just be real for a moment since no one is around to see you nodding in agreement. Maybe you just let life run you over while hiding what you really desire behind statements like, "Well that's just life!" or "I guess it was meant to be that way!" These were the same cowardly excuses Jacob may have used as people ran him over, while draining him of every drop of self worth God created him with.

Are you settling for less than what you desire?

Do you put everyone and everything before yourself every time you have to make a decision?

Do you find yourself waking up to a life other people have lured you into by their wants, accusations and hurts?

If so I have some good news for you. There is hope.

I can sense, even now, your expectation and eagerness to hear what it is going to take for you to begin living your God-given destiny, instead of a life that is centered on pleasing everyone around you. The answer can be found as we look at the life of Jacob, found in our scripture for today.

In this text, we find Jacob – who had left his family, worked fourteen years for the woman of his dreams, inherited a second wife, two concubines and a house full of children, and had his wages changed ten times, only to be blessed by God even more each time – and now he is taking his new family, cattle and all the things he has worked so hard for to a land promised to him by God. When he reaches the edge of the river, he gets word that his brother Esau is coming to kill him and take from him everything he owns. So Jacob once again begins to give up and buckle under the pressures of life. He takes every thing he has, including his wife and kids, and sends them to the other side of the river as a peace offering to his brother Esau.

Yes, once again, wimpy Jacob was accepting whatever came his way.

But this time, something strange happened.

The Bible says that when he was all alone, a man came to him and the two began to wrestle.

I would like to point out a few things about this man.

Number one, the man was a human, but was not a part of Jacob's family, because the Bible said Jacob was "alone." Number two, the man was sent from God, because after the fight was over, the man blessed Jacob, and we know that "every good and perfect gift comes from above." (James 1:17) This "man," which in the Hebrew language translates "mortal," began to fight with Jacob. Something isn't right about this encounter because Jacob never fought for anything. What was it that changed? How did Jacob go from a wimp to a warrior in a moment's time?

I will tell you what I believe happened. I believe Jacob did what you need to do. I believe he got sick and tired of accepting everything that came his way. I believe the man was sent from God to try Jacob and see if he had learned how to be a man. See, what I didn't tell you is that while Jacob was on his journey to live with Laban, he passed by a beautiful stretch of land where he found rest. While he was resting, the Spirit of God came down and told Jacob that He was going to bring Jacob back to this land and give it to him for an inheritance. This is where Jacob was headed when he found himself alone again, wrestling with this man.

Why didn't God just give Jacob the land to begin with? You want to know why? Because it is harder to remain successful than it is to just experience success.

See, God isn't concerned as much about your beginning as He is your ending. This is why you must stay focused on your God-given destiny and never ever give up.

I believe God could not give Jacob the land until he taught Jacob how to stand up and fight for what he desires.

Jacob was almost back at his land of promise when he was confronted, for the final time, with the decision to stand up or to bow down. I believe this man sent from

God came to Jacob and told him to just stay there – just outside the realm of his promises – and God would bless him and his family. I believe the man tried to talk Jacob out of going into his promised land, and just settling once again for second best.

This was the turning point for Jacob, and today must be the turning point for you.

Jacob had had enough. He had gotten to the point where destiny overcame timidity. I believe Jacob told that man as they began to "wrestle" that he was not going to accept any less than what God had promised him. This is the "fight of faith," fighting for what God has promised you.

Fight in the name of Jesus! Fight for your dreams, fight for your desires and fight for you destiny! Grab your sword, man the wall, don't be dismayed by trouble!

And fight!

Ultimately, the truth is, you get what you accept!

Are you fighting or settling?

Remember the words of Nehemiah in 4:14:

"And I looked, and rose up, and said unto the nobles, and to the rulers, and to the rest of the people. Be not afraid of them. Remember the Lord, which is great and terrible, and fight for your brethren, your sons, and your daughters, your wives, and your houses."

"Of all words of tongue or pen, the saddest are these; what might have been." (John Greenleaf Whittier)

How Bad Do You Want It?

"And when he saw that he prevailed not against him..."
Genesis 32:25

————

I believe one of God's biggest questions to us is, "How bad do you want it?"

I mean, for me, there is nothing I dislike more than people who don't stand up for themselves. Think about it, Jesus always stood up for who He was and His purpose. The only reason He died on the cross was because He chose to. Jesus even said, "No one has the power to take my life... I lay it down freely."

This world that we live in takes no prisoners. It is kill or be killed. Conquer or be conquered.

The truth is that if you are going to have anything in this life you are going to have to fight hell and the words of negative people around you to get it. Nothing comes free. Victory over this world even cost God His Son.

I have a question for you: are you ready to fight? Are those dreams on the inside of you important enough to you to break out of your shell and man the walls of battle? God has equipped you with everything you need to prevail. How much easier can it get? Jesus has already pronounced victory. It is time for you to reach out and grab what is rightfully yours. It begins with your willingness to fight.

Jacob was a man who never fought for anything. He was a coward, a wimp, a "prissy-pot," if you will. He was like a dead leaf blown by every wind of change until one day when he got so fed up with weakness that he made a choice to fight back.

That is where you have got to be today. Whether you need to fight for spiritual blessings or worldly desires, it all begins when you choose to fight.

Now I know it is not "spiritually correct" for Christians to fight. Isn't that right? Aren't Christians supposed to always be meek, lowly and searching for the chance to get run over "for the glory of God"? This is the same thinking that got the "hell" beat out of me for so long.

Yes, I said it and I meant it, too. I am writing this chapter engulfed in the angry, warring Spirit of God. I want you to sense the anger and even the plain out hatred toward failure that I have within me by the Spirit of the Lord. You may be thinking, "Jesus never got mad and fought for anything."

I beg to disagree. In Mathew chapter 21, when Jesus entered the temple and saw all the people selling doves and exchanging money, what did He do? The Bible said that Jesus was so angry He threw over their tables and made a whip and began to whip the people and run them out of the temple.

Throughout the Old Testament, our Lord is called the Lord of Hosts. That sounds like a fairly neutral name, because when we think of "hosts" we think of groups, large groups, without any particular contextual meaning. But when we look up the Hebrew word for "hosts" we get much more insight. The Hebrew word is *tsaba*, pronounced tsaw-baw', and meaning a mass of persons, especially people organized for war, an army, or soldiers waiting for warfare.

In scripture, we see the Lord of *Tsaba* often conducting warfare against His enemies and the oppressors of His people. He exhibited that aspect of His being, or what we might call the *Tsaba* spirit, when He drove the moneychangers out of the temple.

Our Lord sounds like a warrior to me.

I don't think that in this instance Jesus would fit into today's description of Christianity, do you?

First of all, we must realize that Jesus had been in that temple many times before. He had seen the people selling animals and exchanging money time and time again. Why, after years of seeing this go on and not doing anything about it, did Jesus on this day begin to war for what He knew to be right?

One thing I would like to point out is what Jesus experienced before He arrived at the temple. He experienced true worship. The Bible says that, as He entered the city, people began to worship Him, crying, "Hosanna to the Son of David!" (v. 9)

They also threw their cloths on the ground for Jesus to ride upon as they waved palm branches in His honor.

One thing that will always create an atmosphere for the "Warrior God," or "*Jehovah Tsaba*," is when you choose to worship Him in the midst of your trial. Something happens within God that triggers an explosion in Him when His people worship Him in the midst of tribulation. If you will just choose to worship Him right now, I believe today God will show up in your life and begin to turn things around for you.

Secondly, I would like to also discuss whom Jesus addressed in the temple and why. The Bible says that Jesus overturned the tables of the oxen, sheep, and dove sellers (John 2:15) as well as the money exchangers.

Let me first deal with the animal sellers.

Why was Jesus so upset with them? It was as much the fact that they were selling animals in the temple as it was *why* they were selling them in the first place.

See, the animals they were selling were animals used in sacrificial offerings unto the Lord. The people of the Bible used to raise the animals that they were going to offer as sacrifices to the Lord. They would nourish the animals, and provide care and love of the animals as their own children from birth. Now, I don't know if you have ever cared for an animal in this way, but if you had, it would be safe to say that you could have an attachment to the animal after all this time and trouble.

This was what the sellers in the temple were doing wrong. They were providing convenience for the people while subverting intimacy with God.

See, God doesn't want you to offer Him anything that isn't precious to you. When dealing with worship, if it doesn't cost you something, He doesn't want it. The people no longer offered to God something that meant something to them. All they had to do, when it came time for a sacrifice, was to buy a blessing from the temple clerk. That infuriated Jesus. To think that intimacy in the temple was replaced by convenience.

Then you have the situation with the money exchangers. Why did Jesus get so upset with them?

For the same reason as with the animal sellers. They were robbing God's people. What they used to do was counter-weight the scales so they would weigh incorrectly. In other words they would set the scales or balance so when the money was weighed out, the exchangers would receive more than was fair.

Financially, the people of God were being robbed.

Let me just say, if you will be faithful to give God what He has designated as His, concerning your finances, He will fight every spirit of poverty that tries to steal your

blessings. That is a promise of God. He said in Malachi
3:10-11:

> *"Bring you all the tithes into the storehouse, that there
> may be meat in mine house, and prove me now
> herewith, says the LORD of hosts, if I will not open
> you the windows of heaven, and pour you out a
> blessing, that there shall not be room enough to
> receive it. And I will rebuke the devourer for your
> sakes, and he shall not destroy the fruits of your
> ground; neither shall your vine cast her fruit before
> the time in the field, says the LORD of hosts."*

God's will is for you to be prosperous! I don't care
what religion says.

Now, there is no excuse for you not to fight for what
God has promised you. We see that even Jesus fought for
what was right. I command you in the Name of Jesus to
be men and women of valor. Fight in Jesus name and with
His authority.

He wants you to win.

The question is, how bad do you want it?

"The human spirit is never finished when it is
defeated; it is finished when it surrenders." (Ben Stein)

The Forming of Generations:

"And when he saw that he prevailed not against him, he touched the hollow of his thigh; and the hollow of Jacob's thigh was out of joint, as he wrestled with him." Genesis 32:25

———

As a father, one of my biggest concerns is how I can help my children live successful lives. I mean, we all should want our children to grow up and have nice things, plenty of money and, most of all, an intimate relationship with God. But the underlying truth is, one day our children will have to begin making decisions on their own and face the consequences to those decisions. So does it really matter how I choose to live my life as their father?

Will the decisions you make today have an effect on the generations of your family tomorrow?

I would like to begin today by looking back at our text and examining what happened to Jacob during his life-changing encounter with God. The Bible says that as Jacob and the man wrestled, the man touched the middle of Jacob's thigh causing it to be displaced.

Now, if you just read this verse as you would a storybook you would simply think Jacob got a "good whupping," as we would say down here in the South.

However, we know that the Word of God is not a simple storybook. It is the inspired Word of the living God! Knowing this I would like to examine the place in Jacob's body where the man chose to affect him from that day forward.

The Bible states that the man specifically caused an everlasting change in Jacob's "thigh." The Hebrew word for thigh is "*yarek*," which translates as the generative parts, or the loins. This, in turn, reveals that the man, whom I believe was sent by God, made an impact not only on Jacob, but his whole lineage to come. From the day Jacob made a decision to stand up for what he desired for his life, his whole blood line was forever changed.

Our choices in life don't only affect us, they affect those around us and those who will come after us. This is even more reason for you to refuse to lose your God-created purpose in life. Your children and your children's children, even to the fourth generation, are depending on you to achieve your purpose in this life.

Let us examine a couple more scriptures so I can break through any false mindset that suggests your choices only affect you.

Genesis 26:18 says:

> "And Isaac *digged again the wells of water, which they had dug in the days of Abraham his father,for* the Philistines had stopped them after the death of Abraham: and he called their names after the names by which his father had called them." (emphasis added)

Here, we read of Isaac and his whole family obtaining nourishment from the life of his father. The root Hebrew word for this word, "well," is "*baar*," which means to engrave or to declare plainly. What this is saying to me is that Isaac received nourishment by what was engraved in and declared plainly through the life of his father.

Isn't that incredible, to know you can dig wells for your children to receive nourishment and instruction!

I encourage you to take the time to dig wells of life for your generations to come.

I don't know about you, but I would rather be the one to experience pain and heartache if I can spare my children from it. I know they will have trials and tribulations, according to John16:33, but the thought that I can declare plainly and provide "wells" for them, so they might not have to go through some of the struggles I have faced in my life, motivates me toward greatness. If you can't get motivated to make something out of your life for you alone, be motivated by knowing your life, whether positive or negative, will effect your generations to follow.

You may be thinking that you have already made too many mistakes and the wells you have dug for your family will spring forth sewage. Let me tell you one thing: that is the very reason God chooses to forget you past – so you can dig new wells for your children. Although God allows us to dig new wells, your children will also receive nourishment from your bad wells, too, if you purify the water.

Let me explain. God will forgive and forget your past, but He will use the wisdom you obtained through the digging process to strengthen your generations to come. For example, let's look at *Joshua 4:21-24*:

"And he spoke unto the children of Israel, saying, When your children shall ask their fathers in time to come, saying, What mean these stones? **Then you shall let your children know** *saying, Israel came over this Jordan on dry land. For the LORD your God dried up the waters of Jordan from before you. Until*

you were passed over, as the LORD your God did to
the Red Sea, which he dried up from before us, until
we were gone over. That all the people of the earth
might know the hand of the LORD that it is mighty:
that you might fear the LORD your God forever."
(emphasis added)

This scripture begins after the children of Israel crossed over the Jordan River and entered into the Promised Land. They were instructed by God to take twelve stones and place them at the place where they crossed the sea, for a reminder of the miracle God did for His people. That is how God gets glory from your "polluted wells," or, in other words, your mistakes in life.

He wants you to help your children through your mistakes. Your children do not need a mom or dad who acts all holy, as if they have never made a mistake before. You may be ashamed of your past; it may be embarrassing and hurtful to bring up your faults, but God will use your past as wells of life and wisdom to your children.

Lay your stones of life out for a memorial to God for His grace and mercy. Let the "limp" you have obtained through the fights in your life be seen by those who love you. You didn't wrestle all night just to obtain the victory for yourself alone. Your life is meant to keep producing life long after you are dead. But no one can live out of a life they did not know. Your children need to be able to relate to you. They can't relate to someone who is always strong, holy and never messes up or has never made mistakes in the past.

They are facing hard decisions, they are experiencing life's choices and letdowns. They will take the advice of someone they can relate to. Don't be fake as you work to be a good parent. Even Jesus showed His scars to a doubting man (Thomas), who happened to be His "son."

The Bible says in Proverbs 20:7 *"The just man walks in his integrity: his children are blessed after him."*

"Wounds breed infection and need to be covered; scars, however, when exposed, bring wisdom and life." (David Edmondson)

The Lie of Jacob:

"And he said unto him, What is thy name? And he said, Jacob." Genesis 32:27

———

If I were to ask you who you are, what would be your reply?

You would probably say something like, "My name is Slick Willie, and I am Jim and Sue's Daddy." This was the kind of answer Jacob gave when the man asked him who he was. He said, "I am Jacob," just as you would identify yourself by your name, occupation, or by the actions of your children.

I am not getting onto you, but at the same time I would like to say that you should not find your self worth in any thing other than who God says you are. God has said you are His friend, His child, His love and the apple of His eye. If you identify yourself under any other title than these, you are bound by the lie of Jacob.

Jacob was caught up in the forming process of this world. He saw himself through what other people called him. See, Jacob translates as "heel catcher," or in other words, "the bottom rung of a ladder."

117

This was the world's view of Jacob. He was nothing, a servant to everyone, someone who would never amount to anything. All of Jacob's life, he lived with this haunting voice directing his every move and thought. No one had to call him worthless or "less than." After all, it seemed to be shouted every time someone called his name.

Can you imagine being awakened every morning to someone calling you worthless? How about if every time you were called to the dinner table, the words seemed to say, "Dinner's ready, you no good servant"?

I don't think these kinds of statements will motivate people to greatness and excellence in everything they set out to do, do you?

Wait one minute, though, before you get down on Jacob, because I want to ask you a question. Or better yet, I would like for you to ask yourself a question. That question is, What kind of things do you allow people to call you? Are you living your life through a worldly classification that isn't lining up with your God-given perspective of who you are? Have those around you guided you to a path that has driven your divine purpose from the highways of your destiny. Are you living a lie?

You may be asking yourself, How do I know if I am living this lie of misinformation?

Together, let's examine a few "names" the world will call you that, if allowed, will camouflage your true identity.

One lie the world around you will tell you is that you are what you do or have done in the past. This could not be any further from the truth. You are not what you do, nor are you what you have done in the past. For instance, if someone has a problem drinking alcohol, we would call him an alcoholic. I mean, that is who he would be, correct? He is an alcoholic because he has a problem with his ability to control a desire to drink alcohol. So he covers his problems with a blanket that will never really keep him warm.

When Adam and Eve sinned in the Garden of Eden, they immediately tried to cover themselves with fig leaves. They covered who they thought they were with something that was dying from the minute they picked it off the vine. This is what we do when we allow ourselves to be categorized by what we have done. When we call ourselves anything other than what God calls us, we've picked the name of something temporal and less than.

The world says, "You are naked," so we make ourselves garments with leaves that are dying as we sew them together. You are not the mistakes you have made. Alcoholic, drug addict, failure, misfit, damaged goods, unfit parent – these are not godly descriptions for who you are. These are worldly categories that confine people and keep them from knowing who God has created them to be.

Decide now, that's not you, not any longer.

I'll ask you the same question God asked Adam after he said he was naked.

"Who told you that you are naked?"

What God was saying was, "You have been naked the whole time and I still communed with you, because you are clothed with My purpose for you. You are arrayed with My grace and love. My purpose for you is not limited to the mistakes you have made. Who has told you that you are insufficient for My presence? Who has told you that who you are is defined by what you are, own or look like? You were not created to live out of your view of who you are, but you are to find hope through My view of you."

This is what God is saying to you every time the world tells you that you are naked. Your response needs to be one like this: "I am naked, but because of God's grace and love for me I am not ashamed for what I have

119

done. I refuse to be covered with your leaves of death and hopelessness, when God has accepted me and created me to be unashamed of my mistakes."

This is the kind of thinking that will bring you strength to continue building your dreams when you have made bad decisions in the past: knowing that you are not your mistakes. You are God's created, chosen, destined child, and it is time for your actions to get in cadence with who God says you are.

Another way we classify who we are is by the successes and failures of our children or protégés. Have you ever heard someone say something like this when asked who he or she is: "I am Jeffery's mom"? This answer would be okay if Jeffery is a rich successful man who is a good father and loves God. Then this mother would feel like she has done a good job. She would have a sense of worth, and this might even motivate her to greater achievements. When this woman is faced with a sense of failure or if she has a letdown in her life, all she would have to do to find strength is to look at her wonderful son.

But what if Jeffery is broke, homeless, addicted to drugs, and maybe has run out on his wife and kid's? What do you think would be this woman's state of mind now? If she classified herself simply as "Jeffery's mom," she would probably feel like a failure and a non-achiever. Every time she sees or even thinks of her son, she might slip into a state of gripping self-hatred and low self-esteem. Her purpose in life might be overshadowed by a lie: "You are Jeffery's mother."

Let me ask you a question while you consider yourself in light of the scenarios given above.

Who changed in those situations? Did the woman change or did Jeffery change?

Jeffery changed, right?

The danger of basing your self worth in those around you is this: if they make good, smart decisions in life, you will have a sense that you are a good person and that you have achieved what God has created you to do. On the other hand, if they choose to make bad decisions and the consequences of those decisions become a life of pain and failure, you will destroy your self worth because of their actions.

You are not what others choose to be!

Try your best to raise your children to love God and make something out of their lives, but who you are cannot be limited to who they choose to be. Jesus poured his life into twelve men; one of them was a devil, one was a liar and a rebel, and the majority of the others were never heard from again after Jesus died. If the Son of God himself had these kinds of odds, what makes you think you are going to do any better?

You are your own person. Be yourself and let God lead you to your destiny.

Finally, the world will try and get you to see yourself through your occupation. For instance, if I were to ask you who you are, you might reply, "I am a construction worker." Or maybe you would say, "I am a teacher at the county school."

If your answer to the question, "Who are you," is confined in your occupation, you are living the lie of Jacob. You are not what you do. If you find your self worth in what you do, what will happen if you get laid off or released from your job? I can tell you what would happen. You would lose your self worth. You would lose your reason for living.

To you, it may seem strange that, just because someone lost his job, he would shut down and refuse to try again, but it happens a lot. The people who fall into this category are called "work-aholics." All they think about is their jobs. They work 100 hours a week, think about work 60 hours a week, and live life the other 8 hours a week. What a dangerous life to live! Don't place your self worth in the hands of a person or a company who will drop you the first time you don't perform.

We wonder why people are always in such a hurry, lying, cheating and fighting for positions and titles. It is not the title people are seeking, it is the lie. The lie of Jacob, that you are who the world around you says you are.

By the Spirit of God, I silence the lie of Jacob in your ear. You are who God says you are! You don't have to perform, you don't have to make all the right decisions, and you don't have to create perfect people around you in order to be who God created you to be. All you have to do is love God, spend time with Him and be willing to be "naked and not ashamed."

This will forever silence the lie of Jacob!

Remember Romans 8:6: *"For to be carnally minded is death; but to be spiritually minded is life and peace."*

"You are who God says you are, you can do what God says you can do, and you can have what God says you can have." (John Osteen)

Prevailing by Your True Identity:

"And he said, Thy name shall be called no more Jacob, but Israel: for as a prince hast thou power with God and with men, and hast prevailed." Genesis 32:28

———

I would like to begin today's study with a question.

Where do you receive your identity? What I mean by that question is, where do you draw purpose in life to keep going when everything around you tells you to quit?

Do you find your self worth in other people's acceptance of you? Do you find fulfillment in money or companionship, or maybe you think you can accomplish your dreams and goals just by receiving a promise from God?

I would like to take a moment and examine the life of Jacob to establish what I believe is the one thing you need in order to always keep striving for success in life, even when failure seems to be your destiny. If you are ready we will begin.

First I would like to deal with the thought that, if people will just accept you and you can just please them, that will be all you need to keep going in life.

When Jacob was a young boy, his father, Isaac, was on his deathbed and Jacob's mother asked Jacob to do something that was dishonest. She told Jacob to dress up like his brother Esau and go into his father's room because, before Isaac died, he would pass down the inherited blessing, and she wanted Jacob instead of Esau to receive the blessing.

So Jacob did what his mother asked him to because, after all, he thought, if I am going to be successful in life I will have to set my desires aside and make everyone else happy.

Guess what! He was wrong!

After Jacob conned his dad into blessing him instead of his brother, his mother kicked him out of the house. That's right, she turned on her son, even though he had done exactly what she had asked.

I would like to tell you something. People are people, and if you are putting your trust, future or emotions in the hands of a sinful man or woman, the only thing you will achieve in life is heartache and lack.

Now don't get me wrong. We need each other, but your heart, trust and decision making should be placed only into the hands of God. He will never fail you. God will never give up on you, and He will never mislead you in any way.

Self worth and strength to conquer the enemies of life cannot and will not come from other people alone.

After Jacob was kicked out of his house, because of one bad decision, he traveled to his uncle Laban's house. On the way, something very wonderful happened to Jacob. As he laid down one night on his journey, the angel of God appeared to him. The angel made him a promise that God would one day give Jacob this land for an inheritance, to him and his children. Jacob named the place Bethel.

I bet you are thinking, "Wow, that would be all I need to accomplish my dreams – to receive a promise from God!"

Guess what: you're wrong!

If all you needed was a promise from God to find purpose in this life, then everyone on this earth would be filled with purpose. You may be asking yourself how I could say that. Well let me just say this: the Bible is in essence a promise from your God to you. Your Father promises victory in every battle, peace through every storm. And He has revealed in Deuteronomy that His will for us is to be successful and prosperous. You have been given many promises from God. So why is failure an option to you? Because you have not found the one key thing that you need in order to find purpose to believe for your promises.

What is that one thing?

Well, hold your horses and I will get to that in one moment.

I will say this: Jacob had a promise from God, but he didn't achieve his destiny until he obtained this one key that I will give you in just a minute. (Aren't you excited?)

First, I want to kick away a big crutch some people like to lean on when they think about how they might realize their dreams in life: MONEY.

How many times have you thought or even said, "If I just had the money, I could accomplish anything"?

Do you know what you have done when you made that statement? You have established that money is bigger, stronger and more reliable than your God.

Jacob may have thought the same thing at one time in his life. When he arrived at Laban's house, Jacob began to work for his uncle. Jacob and Laban agreed on a certain amount of goods or money that Jacob would make every pay period. Now Jacob did not make money like you and I. Instead, in the Bible days they would receive goods such as cattle, sheep, jewels or other things. As Jacob began to work for his uncle, something good began to happen to Jacob, but it wasn't so good for his boss, Laban.

As you may remember, they agreed that every animal with spots on its body would belong to Jacob as his wages. Once this agreement was made, because Jacob was a child of God, every animal that was born had spots on it.

Let me interrupt myself here for a moment and set the record straight. If you are faithful to God, He will be faithful to you. If you will trust God with your tithes, offerings and first fruits, He will bless everything that you do, even down to your great, great, great, great grand children. That is a promise to you from your Father! Trust Him and watch the promotions come.

Let's get back to Jacob. Since animals were being born with spots on them, Laban was losing everything he had and Jacob was becoming rich. So Laban came to Jacob and changed his wages, saying that every animal with stripes on it would be Jacob's wages. Do you know what happened? Beginning at that point, every animal that was born had stripes on it.

Isn't God good?

I said all of that to say this: Jacob had money. He became one of the wealthiest men around. Maybe he thought that money would cover the pain of rejection he had faced and that money is all he needed to be successful in this life.

Guess what: if he did, he was wrong! Jacob was still lonely, rejected and passive. Money was not his answer and money is not your answer.

Next I would like to deal with something else that's not meant to be a springboard to your dreams: companionship. A lot of people think that if they could just find the right person, they could accomplish anything.

Let me start by saying that there is nothing better than having a supportive, loving, caring, encouraging spouse at home, but that is not the key to finding purpose in your life. Jacob worked fourteen years; he was lied to, talked about, and scammed just because he was in love with a woman named Rachel. The Bible says that she was beautiful and pleasant to look at. Jacob and Rachel were created for each other and they were in love. After years of heartache and hard work, Jacob and Rachel were finally married. That was all Jacob thought he needed to find fulfillment in life.

Guess what: he was wrong!

After they were married, Jacob and Rachel realized that she could not bear children. She was no longer this perfect good-looking woman. She had faults. It wasn't long before Jacob found out that his purpose in life could not come from just loving, and being in love with an imperfect person. People, no matter how much love is involved, will hurt other people's feelings.

If you are finding your purpose in life through companionship, you will lose that purpose as soon as you realize that companion's imperfections.

So what is the key thing you need in order to find your purpose in life and to give you strength to overcome every obstacle that stands in your way?

I believe the one thing a person needs to find purpose in life was the very thing Jacob received from the man he wrestled with all night. That one blessing was his "true identity."

Wow! Amazing! What a wonderful revelation, you may be thinking. Well, let's take a moment and just see how great a revelation it really is.

The man asked Jacob – who had tried to find his purpose and strength to succeed in so many things he did not know what to do – "What is your name?" In other words, he was asking, "Who are you?"

127

Jacob said, "I am Jacob," which, we established in the last chapter, was a lie. Jacob did not know it was a lie, but it was. That was the name his parents gave him, and it was the name people called him, but that was not who God said he was.

The man looked at Jacob and said, "You are not Jacob, you are Israel." At that moment, Jacob obtained his true identity.

Your true identity is not who this world says you are, but who God says you are. Jacob translates as "heel catcher," but Israel translates as "prince of God."

Your problem is that you are walking around trying to find purpose by living out the desires of someone you are not. What I mean to say is, you are not who you see every time you look in the mirror. You are not the person everyone sees or who people call you. Who you are is found in the identity of your spirit because God is a Spirit and we were created in His image and in His likeness. Therefore, we are spirit beings. We are spirits, we have a soul (mind, will, and emotions) and we live in a body. You must grasp the ability to trust the voice that comes from the real you.

Let's go deeper into this revelation and see what God has painted for us. The man sent from God identified two separate individuals, Jacob and Israel. Now, both were in one body, but two identities were established. Don't misunderstand me. I am not saying we all have multiple personalities, but even Paul wrote in Romans chapter 7 of the war between his "spirit man" and his "flesh man."

It is vital to your Christian life to learn how to distinguish the voice of your spirit (who you are) and the voice of your flesh (who you see in the mirror).

The Bible makes it clear that we will be confronted on any given day by one of three separate voices. First and foremost, there is the voice of God. The voice of God is always in communion with the spirit of "new born" Christians.

The Bible states in 1 John 2:20, *"But ye have an unction from the Holy One, and you know all things."*

This scripture is talking about your spirit. As a Christian, the real you always knows the correct thing to do in every situation because it is in constant communion with God through the Holy Spirit. Your task and challenge is to only listen to the voice of God, which speaks through the voice of your spirit, or what I like to call "the voice of Israel."

The voice of Israel is the voice of who you really are, the voice of your spirit. This voice can be identified by one distinguishing characteristic. That is, the voice of Israel will always be in line with the God's Word and it will always reveal who God is. In other words, the voice of your spirit, which is who God created you to be, will always guide you by the Word of God and the Attributes of God, and this voice will always bring you purpose.

The voice of Israel, which is your spirit, will never condemn you because that is not an attribute of God. The voice of Israel will never tempt you with evil because God does not tempt with evil. The voice of Israel will never lead you astray because that is not what God does. The key to finding purpose and strength in this life comes when you can identify who you really are and the voice in which your spirit communicates.

The voice of Israel, my friend, is the voice you want to heed. It is your voice. It is God's voice. It is the voice of your true identity.

The other two voices you must deal with are the voice of the devil, which isn't hard to recognize, and the voice of your flesh, which I like to call the "voice of Jacob."

The devil's voice or the voice of his demonic cohorts always speaks of lack, destruction, condemnation and perversion. That is who he is, so that is what he says. The voice of your flesh, or the "voice of Jacob," on the other hand is a little more cunning. The voice of Jacob is speaking to you ninety-five percent of the time. I know we blame the devil for everything bad, but I encourage you to search the scriptures and find out what the Bible says about your flesh. A good place to start would be in Galatians 5:19-23 as it lists the lusts of your flesh.

The voice of Jacob, your flesh, can be identified when you realize the flesh wants to do four main things. One, it always wants to make you seem weak.

Romans 7:18 says,

"For I know that in me (that is, in my flesh,) dwelleth no good thing: for to will is present with me; but how to perform that which is good I find not."

The voice of the flesh always seems to shout, "I Can't!" anytime God, your friends, or our boss asks you to do something over and above what you have ever done before. Your "Jacob" yells, "You can't do that; you will fail!"

The second thing the voice of your flesh does is cry out for the law. It rebukes the thought of grace and mercy. It always wants you to prove by your actions that you are saved and in love with God. Law, Law, Law is what pleases your flesh.

Romans 7:5 says,

"I thank God through Jesus Christ our Lord. So then with the mind I myself serve the law of God; but with the flesh the law of sin."

The third thing the voice of your flesh does is to try to pervert the voice of God.

Galatians 5:17&18 says,

"For the flesh lusteth against the Spirit, and the Spirit against the flesh: and these are contrary the one to the other: so that ye cannot do the things that ye would. But if ye be led of the Spirit, ye are not under the law."

When God promises you something, the voice of the flesh will always make you get in a hurry. It will take a part of what God is saying to you and make it fit your fleshly desires. The voice of your flesh always perverts what God is trying to tell you.

Lastly, the voice of your flesh, or the voice of Jacob, will never be silenced. So you'd better learn how to identify it and close its mouth!

2 Corinthians 10:3-5 says,

"For though we walk in the flesh, we do not war after the flesh. For the weapons of our warfare are not carnal, but mighty through God to the pulling down of strong holds; Casting down imaginations, and every high thing that exalteth itself against the knowledge of God, and bringing into captivity every thought to the obedience of Christ;"

The key to total freedom is to obtain your true identity. This is not a one-time achievement, but an every-moment endeavor. Your true identity is "Israel," not "Jacob." Each has a voice. Each has a name. Each has a purpose. You are "Israel."

Listen to your voice, the voice of Israel, and you will never quit, withdraw or feel worthless again.

1 Corinthians 5:17-21 says,

"Therefore if any man be in Christ, he is a new creature: old things are passed away; behold, all things are become new. And all things are of God,

131

who hath reconciled us to himself by Jesus Christ, and hath given to us the ministry of reconciliation. To wit, that God was in Christ, reconciling the world unto himself, not imputing their trespasses unto them; and hath committed unto us the word of reconciliation. Now then we are ambassadors for Christ, as though God did beseech you by us: we pray you in Christ's stead, be ye reconciled to God. For he hath made him to be sin for us, who knew no sin; that we might be made the righteousness of God in him."

"My true identity is the fingerprint of God on my life." (David Edmondson)

He Chose You in Spite of You:

"Yet now hear, O Jacob my servant; and Israel, whom I have chosen." Isaiah 44:1

———

Have you ever wanted to do something that was good and honorable and you failed to go through with it? Or have you ever wanted to, or had the desire to, do something that was wrong or a sin, but you didn't because you just couldn't go through with it? Are these times not mind-boggling and at the same time somewhat amazing?

It almost seems as though there are two of you fighting against each other. It is kind of like that old cartoon. You know the one where an angel is sitting on one shoulder telling the character to do good, but on the other shoulder is what looks like a devil trying to persuade the character to do evil.

Let me go ahead and tell you, when this happens (which is all the time) you are not a psychotic, demon-possessed, bad person. You are a righteous redeemed spirit living in a sinful, evil, fleshly body.

Paul dealt with this same thing in Romans 7:18-23:

"I know that nothing good lives in me, that is, in my sinful nature. For I have the desire to do what is good, but I cannot carry it out. For what I do is not the good I want to do; no, the evil I do not want to do--this I keep on doing. Now if I do what I do not want to do, it is no longer I who do it, but it is sin living in me that does it. So I find this law at work: When I want to do good, evil is right there with me. For in my inner being I delight in God's law, but I see another law at work in the members of my body, waging war against the law of my mind and making me a prisoner of the law of sin at work within my members."

So don't feel bad when such evil thoughts arise in your mind or when you just get out of church and you all of a sudden do something you just repented of doing. Today, I would like to show you how God deals with you – I mean each of you: who you really are, which is spirit, and what you are, which is a sinful fleshly being.

First, I would like to deal with "Jacob." In our scripture today, God calls Jacob His servant. As we have already discussed, Jacob is a representation of your flesh. God goes a little further and identifies Jacob, or the flesh, as His servant. What I would like to say here is that the "good fight of faith" (1 Timothy 6:12) is the warfare of "casting down imaginations," making your rebellious, fleshly mind and voice submit, or be a servant to God and His will.

I heard someone say once, "You may not be able to prevent a pigeon from landing on your head, but you can keep him from building a nest there."

This is a warfare that you will be fighting until you die or Jesus comes back. You will think impure thoughts at times, but it is your job to kill them before conception.

You will always have miscues and sin in your life, but it is your assignment to repent and purpose not to do them again. This is all God expects from your "Jacob." God knew when Adam sinned that the separation between Him and mankind would always be there in the flesh until His final return. That is the reason God will give us a new "glorified body" when we get to Heaven, so sin cannot reign in our flesh any longer. But until then, we have been commanded by God to make our fleshly mind, will and voice become as a servant to God.

God looks at our flesh and its actions through the eyes of a master watching His servant. This is why, when we allow our flesh to do its own will and not serve the will of God, there is a consequence. After all, any servant that is disobedient learns obedience through punishment. But thank God that His grace and mercy steps in just in the nick of time to pay the eternal price for the sins of my Jacob!

According to 1 John 1:9,

"If we confess our sins, he is faithful and just to forgive us our sins, and to cleanse us from all unrighteousness."

God is faithful even when Jacob isn't.

The fact remains that Jacob can never and will never become a complete and loyal servant to God. The Bibles says in Romans 8:7 & 8,

"Because the carnal mind is enmity against God. For it is not subject to the law of God, neither indeed can be. So then they that are in the flesh cannot please God."

It is impossible for your "Jacob" and your God to be friends. The relationship between God and Jacob is that of Master and servant. It was from that kind of relationship that God spoke these words in Leviticus 11:45:

"You shall therefore be holy, for I am holy."

He was commanding us to make our Jacobs become servants to God, because you can always tell what kind of man the master is by watching the servant.

Again I say, thank God for His grace and His mercy! 2 Corinthians 4:16 states,

"For which cause we faint not; but though our outward man (Jacob) *perish, yet the inward man* (Israel) *is renewed day by day."*

Just as God identifies Jacob as His servant, He then identifies Israel as His chosen one. Thank God that you are God's pick! Though your flesh is His servant, the real you is His chosen one. He looks at you through the eyes of love.

I like to explain it like this. Where I live, in Gainesville, Georgia, almost every weekend someone is having a yard sale. This, of course, is when a family or a group of families get all of their "hand me downs," better known as junk, and they sell it to the public on their front lawn or driveway. You can buy shirts for a quarter, pants for a dollar, toys for fifty cents and things like that. Basically, it is when people clean out their attic, and they don't want to throw away the stuff, so they sell it for the lowest price they can live with.

When the Bible says that God chooses you, it is like He goes to a yard sale and when he gets there, he asks the homeowner, "What is the most worthless, cheapest piece of junk you have?" The homeowner then shows God this worn out, beat up and rusted tin can.

God, in turn, looks at the man and says, "This is what I want and I will pay you $1 million for it."

This doesn't sound too logical, does it?

136

I mean, no one in his or her right frame of mind would pay that kind money for an old piece of junk. This is what makes being chosen by God so good, because, on the outside, you just look like a sinful, beat up, worn out servant, but on the inside you are "Israel," a prince with the favor of God. He has picked you up off the yard sale table.

No, as a matter of fact He picked up out of the trash, because you were not even worth being placed on the table. The yard sale owner took one look at you and thought, "I won't even be able to give this away for a penny. It isn't worth my time to clean it up and put it with the other junk!"

Thank God, when the world sees your Jacob and casts a judgment of death on you, God chooses to look at your Israel. He then makes the choice to pick you up, take you home and create out of you something that the world could not have imagined was possible.

This is the way God chooses to look at a born-again Christian, even when his or her "Jacob" acts like a rebellious servant. The Israel in you attracts God's presence to you.

It is kind of like the story of Hagar and Ishmael. Hagar, being the servant and handmaiden of Abraham and Sarah, was the perfect servant. She was the perfect woman – perfect in her loyalty, honesty and faithfulness. But she had a son named Ishmael, who was imperfect because he was her seed and not the seed of Sarah, God's chosen woman. Although he was perfect through Abraham, because God called Abraham the perfect seed, he was imperfect through Hagar because Sarah was Abraham's perfect wife, not Hagar. (I hope that all makes sense so far.)

Well, anyway, one day Hagar and Ishmael were sent away to live in a wilderness because Sarah was jealous of Ishmael, her handmaiden's son. To make a long story short, while Hagar and Ishmael were in the wilderness, they ran out of food and water. So Hagar took her child, Ishmael, and placed him under a bush and left him, because she did not want to hear him cry as he died of starvation and dehydration. She then walked away from her child and began to cry out to God.

So you must understand that there were now two separate voices crying in the wilderness. There was the voice of Hagar, the example of perfection, loyalty and faithfulness, as well as the voice of Ishmael, which was the voice of imperfection, rejection and failure.

As these two distinct voices cried out to God, the angel of the Lord appeared to Hagar and said,

> "*What aileth thee, Hagar? Fear not; for God hath heard the voice of the lad where he is.*" (Genesis 21:17)

The amazing thing I would like to point out is the fact that God did not hear nor respond to the voice off perfection, but He responded to the voice of imperfection. It was not the voice of the perfect, loyal, honest person that attracted the presence of God, but rather the voice of the imperfect, rejected seed of a slave. The fact is God is attracted to you because your Jacob needs Him and your Israel desires Him.

Without imperfection you could stand alone. You wouldn't need God. It is not your perfection that attracts God to you. It is your imperfections. If you were holy, perfect and righteous in and of yourself, you wouldn't need God.

But you're not! And you do!

Do you notice the Bible never says that God is the God of Abraham, Isaac and Israel? It says God is the God of Abraham, Isaac and Jacob! This is because God is the God of the worst of you, not the best of you!

I challenge you to allow your Jacob to draw you closer to God instead of pushing you away from God. God desires you just as you are. Your Jacob and you as Israel!

"The ultimate measure of a man is not where he stands in moments of comfort and convenience, but where he stands at times of challenge and controversy." (Martin Luther King Jr.)

The Second Forming Process:

"Thus saith the LORD that made thee, and formed thee from the womb, which will help thee. Fear not, O Jacob, my servant; and thou, Jesurun, whom I have chosen."
Isaiah 44:2

————

If you recall, on days twelve through eighteen we examined Jeremiah chapter one. This is where we dealt with what I have entitled, "The First Forming Process." We talked about how, before God created you in your mother's womb, He created your destiny. We learned that God did not create a destiny for you, but rather, you for a destiny. Then while you were in your mother's womb, God equipped you with everything you will ever need to accomplish the destiny you were created for.

Next, we dealt with the fact, that after we were created for a destiny and after God equipped us to accomplish that destiny, God then pushed us forth into this world to be victorious in all of our endeavors.

If you can remember what was in those chapters, you are now ready for the final three days of your encounter with who God created you to be. If not, you may want go back and study again the truths found in those chapters. It

141

is very important for you to receive what God has for you over the next three days.

If you are ready, let's wrap this bad boy up and begin to live out our lives "formed," the way God intended for us to be.

In our scripture text for today, we read of God addressing Jacob and Israel once again. The Lord makes a statement that will give us deeper insight into the way God views us as His creation and children. The Lord looked at Jacob-Israel and said, "I made you and then I formed you *FROM* the womb..." He then goes on to establish a difference, once again, between Jacob and Israel.

I would like to ask you once more to go back and examine our scripture for today, and as you do, look at the sentence structure God used in speaking to His creation. Notice that God said first, I made thee, and, second, He said I formed thee. Later in the sentence, He addresses Jacob and, afterward, Israel. (Jesurun is a term of endearment applied to Israel meaning "upright.")

From this sentence structure we can draw the conclusion that God was first saying He created Jacob. Then, because God said second, "I formed you from the womb," and addressed Israel, we can conclude that God was telling Israel that he was "formed."

It is important that we see the difference between His creating and forming acts. God reveals it this way so we can identify the difference between creating our flesh, our Jacob (what we are), and forming our spirit, our Israel, (who we are).

I hope and pray this is all making sense to you. If not, go back and read this paragraph until it gels. If we are "tracking," just continue in faith.

First, I would like you to see what God is revealing about Jacob, or, in other words, our flesh. God told Jacob that He created him. Because of this we know that God is talking about the fleshly man. I say that because the Bible says God created man out of the dust of the ground. This was when God created mankind's physical body. We must understand that God establishes a difference between our flesh and our spirit.

I'm being careful to repeat this because I want you to be able to grasp this revelation of who you are and how God sees you.

God created our flesh out of dirt. The fact is, our flesh is nothing more than, and will never be anything more than, dirt. Where we go wrong as Christians is, we see ourselves through the acts and the limitations of our flesh, so we think that God views us through those same eyes. It is very important for you to know that, as long as you live in this earthly, dirt vessel, you will fail. This is the nature of your flesh: nasty, dirty, and ugly.

The good news is that God can distinguish between your fleshly Jacob and your spirit Israel. He created your Jacob; it is established in what it is. No matter how much you pray, fast or study, your flesh will always be flesh. God chooses to put up with our dirty old Jacob, because He wants so much to commune with our Israel.

Isn't that remarkable?

If you haven't received anything from this book to this point, or if you don't get anything from the rest of this book, that one statement was worth the price you paid for this book. Just so you won't forget it, I'm summarizing it in large type:

God loves and desires the real you so much He chooses to overlook the part of you that hates His presence.

So He created the flesh, the temporal, but He formed your spirit, the part of you that will live forever.

God addressed Jacob; then He addressed Israel.

God told Israel that he was not created, but rather, he was formed. Not only that, but God had been forming him "from" the womb. This is the second forming process.

Let me explain it this way: God did not just create you for a destiny, equip you for that destiny and then push you toward that destiny. He goes beyond, and helps you along the way. God is saying to His creation, "You are too important to Me not to achieve your destiny. So, as you go through this life, bound up in the created, dirty, fleshly Jacob, know that I am forming your Israel every day. I am forming you through trials, failures, successes and victories. Did I not promise you that "all things will work together for your good"? (Romans 8:28)

Can you receive what God is trying to say to you today?

You did not just come across this book for no reason. God planned in your destiny, at this time in your life, for you to receive the breath of His word through this study.

God did not just create you and throw you out into the deep, raging waters of this life to sink and drown. He is with you every moment of every day. There is nothing you have faced or ever will face in this life that God has not allowed to come your way. If you know and believe this, you can face anything.

Also, you must understand that through whatever you are facing today, God's hands are forming you into your desires. The Bible says in Psalms 37 that God will give you the desires of your heart. For God to bless you with the desires of you heart, He first has to purify your heart, and then get you to the place where you can handle what God blesses you with.

God is so good!!!

Before we finish with today's devotion, I would like to give you one more insight into the way God communicates with your Israel (the real you, your spirit).

144

In Isaiah 44: 2, you will notice that God calls Israel by the name "Jesurun." Jesurun is a poetic term for the name Israel. So, what God was doing in this verse as He addressed Israel was, He was singing Israel a love ballad.

My friend, listen to this man of God as I tell you this: God sings love songs over you every moment of your life. He is not mad at you. He does not want to put sickness on you. God is neither angry with you, nor is He displeased with you. I don't care the mistakes your Jacob has made. God is still writing poems and ballads to you, His bride.

Check out what the writer of the Song of Solomon writes in chapter 2 when dealing with God and the way He desires to be with us:

"I am a rose of Sharon, a lily of the valleys (This is Jesus*). Like a lily among thorns is my darling among the maidens. Like an apple tree among the trees of the forest is my lover among the young men. I delight to sit in his shade, and his fruit is sweet to my taste. He has taken me to the banquet hall, and his banner over me is love. Strengthen me with raisins; refresh me with apples, for I am faint with love. His left arm is under my head, and his right arm embraces me. Daughters of Jerusalem, I charge you by the gazelles and by the does of the field: Do not arouse or awaken love until it so desires. Listen! My lover! Look! Here he comes, leaping across the mountains, bounding over the hills. My lover is like a gazelle or a young stag. Look! There he stands behind our wall, gazing through the windows, peering through the lattice. My lover spoke and said to me, 'Arise, my darling, my beautiful one, and come with me. See! The winter is past; the rains are over and gone. Flowers appear on the earth; the season of singing has come, the cooing of doves is heard in our land. The fig tree forms its early fruit; the blossoming vines spread their*

fragrance. Arise, come, my darling; my beautiful one, come with me.' My dove in the clefts of the rock, in the hiding places on the mountainside, show me your face let me hear your voice; for your voice is sweet, and your face is lovely. Catch for us the foxes, the little foxes that ruin the vineyards, our vineyards that are in bloom. My lover is mine and I am his; he browses among the lilies. Until the day breaks and the shadows flee, turn, my lover, and be like a gazelle or like a young stag on the rugged hills."

This is how the Father thinks of you. You are His bride and no one marries someone he is not attracted to. God thinks you are *fine!* (As we would say in Georgia.)

Now, I know the religious part of your Jacob wants you to throw this book down and never open it again, but I encourage you to listen to your Israel. Let the real you be held in the arms of your bridegroom. This is how God forms you from the womb. When you are feeling lonely, abused, worthless, hopeless and distraught, God pulls you into His lap and forms you with the words of life and love from His lips.

This is the God you serve and this is the Father who has chosen you just as you are. Every day through every situation, God is forming you into who you desire to be, which is who He has destined you to become. You can't lose! Not with a Groom who will never leave you and never forsake you! He has chosen you! To Him, nothing compares to you!

"Help! My new heart is living in an old body!" (Bishop T. D. Jakes)

I Am Glorious in God's Sight:

"And now, saith the LORD that formed me from the womb to be his servant, to bring Jacob again to him. Though Israel be not gathered, yet shall I be glorious in the eyes of the LORD, and my God shall be my strength." Isaiah 49:5

––––––––

I would like to address the question most asked by Christians all around the world. That question is, "How can a Holy God love, respect, honor and desire to have an intimate relationship with me, a sinful man or woman?"

This question can be answered as we examine our scripture reference for today. The Lord shows us how He deals with our Jacob, who we know to be our flesh, and with our Israel, which is our spirit.

First, the Lord deals with the servant man, which is Jacob, or your flesh.

The Lord said to Jacob, "I have been forming you to be my servant, to bring you again to me." God shows us here that He understands that our flesh does not want to have a relationship with Him. God knows our flesh has to be made to serve Him. He also shows us His grace here;

because He goes on to say that His will is "...to bring Jacob back to Himself."

You may be asking yourself, what does He mean by all of this?

Let me explain. There is nothing about you that can be hidden from God. He "understands your thoughts from far off." He knows everything about you, and through His grace and mercy He draws your Jacob to Himself.

Here God reveals a very important key for us to walk in victory every day of our lives. That key is that your Christian walk, with regard to your flesh, is a process. God told Jacob that He was bringing him back to Himself, through a process of making Jacob to be His servant. To you, God is saying He knows your faults, He understands you have evil thoughts and fleshly desires, but He wants you to live free from condemnation, knowing that He is bringing your evil flesh back to Himself. God understands that this is a process, and process takes time.

I say to you by the Spirit of God, "Don't get in a hurry."

Do you remember when King David was going to kill Goliath? (1 Samuel 17) In this story, David, a young shepherd boy, went out to fight against a huge warrior named Goliath. Now, when Goliath saw this little boy, between the ages of 12 and 15, coming to fight him, he became angry. If that wasn't enough, this cocky little boy was only equipped with a slingshot and a few rocks.

The point I would like to make here is found in 1 Samuel 17:49:

> *"And David put his hand in his bag, and took thence a stone, and slang it, and smote the Philistine in his forehead, that the stone sunk into his forehead; and he fell upon his face to the earth."* (emphasis added)

Do you realize that, for David to be able to strike Goliath in his forehead, something very unusual had to happen? In Bible days, the armies were set up with "armor bearers" and soldiers. It was the armor bearer's duty to stay in front of the soldier to protect him while in battle. The shields that the armor bearers carried were tall enough to extend from the soldier's head to his feet.

Now, Goliath was approximately eight feet tall. Can you imagine how heavy his shield was? Theologians say that, because David was very young and because he was only armed with a sling and rocks, Goliath got so mad that he ran toward David. Goliath, being so big, outran his armor bearer. For that reason, David could strike him with his stone in a place that would usually have been protected.

So I say to you, "Don't outrun your armor bearer!" Allow God to draw your Jacob back to Himself. God's promise to you is that He will stay true to the process. (Philippians 1:6)

The problem, however, is not with God, but rather with us. He stays true to the process, but we often cannot deal with the fact that our Jacob rebels, withdraws and fails God every day. God chooses to deal with our Jacob through the process of time, but we get in a hurry and condemnation brings the process to a screeching halt.

The Lord goes on to say in verse 5 of Isaiah 49 (I'm paraphrasing), "Though Israel is not with me, I shall be his strength." What does God mean here?

What He is saying is that God is drawing Jacob back to Himself, and though Israel (your spirit) is somewhat away from God because of your sinful flesh, God will strengthen Israel.

I hope you can now see what makes the forming process work. God deals with or convicts your flesh. He does this to draw your flesh back to Him to serve Him. God knows, however, that this will take time – and actually will never completely happen until we receive our glorified bodies in heaven – but He sticks to the process anyway. As God draws your Jacob back to Himself, He strengthens Israel to stand in God's grace and mercy as holy, righteous and acceptable in His presence.

This should bring you victory today, knowing that even when your Jacob fails you, your Israel stands strong.

This process can only be stopped by one thing. That one thing is, if Israel is overtaken or begins to think like Jacob – a servant and not a son.

The Bibles says in Proverbs 18:14,

> *"The spirit of a man will sustain his infirmity; but a wounded spirit who can bear?"*

This scripture describes this forming process precisely. Your spirit will fight against the voice of your Jacob. It will fight against the sickness of your sinful flesh, but if you ever allow your Israel to listen to your Jacob, it will become wounded.

What does this scripture say about a wounded spirit? "Who can bear it?" In other words, if your Israel ever becomes convinced that there is no difference between him and Jacob, the process is over. This is why it is very important to understand the difference between the voice of your Jacob and the voice of your Israel. Jacob will always speak against the things of God and Israel will always speak the truth about God and His will for your life.

If your Israel ever becomes convinced that there is no difference between him and Jacob, the process is over.

This is the second forming process in a nutshell. This process takes time. As a matter of fact, it will take the rest of your life. But the truth is, you can live every second in the victory of God even while in the middle of this forming process, if you can tell the difference between the voice of Jacob and the voice of Israel.

The reason I can make the statement that you can live in victory every moment of your life is because of what Jacob said at the end of our scripture. Jacob said, "My God shall be my strength." The strength you need for total victory through the forming process of life comes from God. This is how it works. The Holy Spirit of God communes with your Israel. During this communion, strength is given to Israel, the real you, your spirit. This strength from God, given to your Israel through intimate communion with Him, gives you the power to bring your Jacob into the servanthood of God.

In other words, God's strength is given to Israel to keep Jacob in line. If Israel ever becomes weaker than Jacob, Israel will be "wounded." This is why your daily quiet time with God is so vital. Not so you can please God, talk God into blessing you, or to make God love and use you. Your intimate time with God is to bring strength to your Israel so that Israel can overcome Jacob. This is why we read our Bibles, pray, fast, witness and do what God asks us to do. Not so we can "get in good with the Boss man," but so we can make it through the forming process victoriously.

What a liberating thought!

Quit going through some old tired routine, trying to impress God enough to use you. He has already created you; He has created you for a destiny, equipped you and is providing you with the strength to be formed into His image again. This has already been done.

Your time with God can't be relegated and restricted to a daily routine, part of a schedule you set to accommodate your needs and activities. Now I know it is good to have routine times you set aside for prayer, but sometimes God wants to spend time with you when *He* wants to. It is not all about the time; it is all about the call.

We please our Jacob when we have the attitude, "Praise God, I spent an hour in prayer and study today!" Your Jacob is so happy because you have satisfied "the Law." But sometimes the Lord says to you, "Yeah, that was your hour, but I called you later in the day and the football game on TV was more important to you."

Your Israel will not get caught up in worldly times and seasons; it is listening for the call from God! Don't get caught up in the doctrines and laws of men and women to please your Jacob. Do you know why I say this? Because, if you dance to the tune of your demanding flesh, it won't be long before your time set aside will not be enough, because your Jacob will always condemn you with "more time, more sacrifice."

1 Samuel 15:22 says, *"Behold, to obey is better than sacrifice..."* To obey the call of God to stop what you are doing and come into His presence is better than sacrificing your scheduled time everyday, just to please your flesh. That is the Word of God, not the traditions of men.

We preach how God has freed us from the law (Galatians 3:13), but then we allow our Jacob to bring us back into the bondage from which Christ has made us free.

I will finish with these statements for all you who still feel the need to appease your Jacob with timelines, structured prayers and holy places:

"Where the Spirit of the Lord is, there is liberty." (2 Corinthians 3:17)

"Not that we are sufficient of ourselves to think any thing as of ourselves; but our sufficiency is of God." (2 Corinthians 3:5)

"If the Son therefore shall make you free, you shall be free indeed." (The Bible: John 8:36)

Your First Breath:

*"And when he had said this, he **breathed on them**, and saith unto them, Receive ye the Holy Ghost:"* John 20:22

———

How do you see yourself now? I mean, now that you know you are not a mistake. Now that you know you are the image of God and the likeness of God in this world. 1 John 4:17 states,

*"Herein is our love made perfect, that we may have boldness in the Day of Judgment: **because as he (Jesus) is, so are we in this world**."* (Emphasis added)

I hope and pray that somewhere throughout the pages of this devotion, you have found *you*. The thing that will make Christianity successful is when Christians act like the men and women God has made us through the blood of Jesus. You are redeemed, sanctified, holy, righteous, perfected, honorable, forgiven, accepted, destined, a saint – and you are able to make mistakes without losing any of these qualities.

This is who you are. This is the grace and mercy of God, through Jesus, sealed by the Holy Spirit, freely given to you.

You are created in the image and likeness of God. Your body is the temple of the Holy Spirit. (1 Corinthians 6:19) You have a destiny, prepared and declared by God, drawing you to itself.

Begin to chase your dreams. Every desire you have in your heart that is in harmony with God's Word for your life will come to pass. The Bible says in 2 Corinthians 1:20 that the promises of God are "yes and Amen!" This means that there are two places of promise for you. The first is the "place of yes." This is the place where God makes His promise spoken into your life known to you. This is like a commercial. God gives you a taste of what is to come, and you know what the Bible says about those who hunger and thirst after righteousness. *They shall be filled*, according to Matthew 5:6. This taste will keep you going in the dark times. This taste will give you strength in the toughest wars of your life. This taste in the end will give birth to your destiny.

The second "place of promise" is the "place of Amen." This is when your promise is revealed in the flesh, or what I like to call the "third dimension." This place is known by its dramatic, sudden, unexpected change. When the timing of your promise arrives at the "place of Amen," there is no time to pray, fast or figure it out, it just happens.

The hard thing for us is the transition period from the place of yes and the place of Amen. Did you know that the longest and most severe time of a woman's birthing labor is called the transition period? This is the time when the baby, or the gift of God, transitions into the birth canal. The baby will die in the birth canal if the mother doesn't have the strength to push. In birthing God's promises to you, the strength to "push" comes from knowing, beyond a shadow of doubt, who God has created you to be.

The next thing that is good to know is that God is continually forming you into who God had destined you to be. God has never given up on you, and He never will. That is so hard for you to comprehend, I know, because of this world we live in. Everyone has been let down, lied to and forsaken by close friends and families.

The thing is, though, God is not of this world. God told Moses, when He commanded him to go to Pharaoh, to tell Pharaoh "I am" sent him. God was saying that everything you need at anytime in your life, He Is! This, my friend, has nothing to do with you; it is all about "I am."

I would like to close with my last word from God to you. Actually, I want to release you to do something in the spirit that you may have never really done before.

Since you know who God has created you to be, you know you have a purpose in life, and you have found out that God cares enough about you to put up with you, now you can be released.

Released to do what?

I release you, in Jesus' name, to take your first breath. Breathe in and take your first real breath in a life of purpose and freedom. Take your first breath in a world of ease and faith in who you are in Christ Jesus.

"Take your first breath my child and never be suffocated again by the cares of life and traditions of men again," says Your Father, the Great I Am.

Galatians 2:20-21: "*I am crucified with Christ: nevertheless I live; yet not I, but Christ lives in me: and the life which I now live in the flesh I live by the faith of the Son of God, who loved me, and gave himself for me. I do not frustrate the grace of God: for*

157

if righteousness come by the law, then Christ has died in vain."

"The life of the flesh is in the blood, but the life of the spirit is in the breath." (David Edmondson)